FOLLOW
YOUR
FERNWEH

KINDLE SMYTH

FOLLOW YOUR FERNWEH

DISCOVER A REGULAR PATH TO
AN EXTRAORDINARY LIFE

Follow Your Fernweh by Kindle Smyth

Published by Kaleo Publishing
Medford, MA

www.followyourfernweh.com

Copyright © 2021 by Kindle Smyth

Cover by 100 Covers
Author cover photo by Ana Pavesi Studio
Edited by Chelsea Slade

ISBN: 979-8-9853785-0-4 (print)
ISBN: 979-8-9853785-1-1 (ebook)

Printed in the United States of America

First Edition

Contents

fernweh (n.) German: a longing for distant places

Introduction

Hiya. Or, hiyeeee! (whichever suits you)

So glad you are here. Literally, so, so glad. You finding this book is an answer to prayer—my prayers for both you and for me. This book has been a lifetime in the making, followed by a few years of the "experiencing and refining" process.

You might be wondering straight away what *fernweh* is, and I'll explain that more fully in the first part of the book, but, ultimately, it's a word I've borrowed from German to help explain a feeling—a longing—I've had my whole life.

A few years ago, I hit a crossroads, which prompted me to follow a desire to travel that always lived below the surface of my day-to-day life. I left my home of fifteen years, put my things in storage, and spent an entire year traveling the globe. This started an unbelievable season of growth, one that reshaped my entire life.

My personal journey includes travel, but this is not a travel book, per se. This is a book for all those in search of a sweeter, deeper, and more impactful life.

My hope is that as we explore the idea of fernweh, it will give you a way to describe the many different types of longing that have been growing inside your soul for a while, too. Whatever that dream is that you've been pushing aside, that goal that feels out of reach, that destination you've longed to visit—get ready to uncover it, chase it, and start living your life out loud.

Our journey is broken into five stages that I experienced in the process of following my fernweh: Discover, Plan, Enjoy, Guard, and Expand. My goal is to help you discover, refine, and eventually follow your own fernweh—whatever that may be. It's a journey we get to explore together, one I know will result in transformation.

You see, I learned a few important lessons during my year of travel and since, and the more I shared my story, the more I saw its impact on others. What you'll find here is my personal experience of chasing a dream—following a calling—mixed with some aspirational ideas and practical tips you can use on your own adventure through life. I also share stories that include the unique and inspiring people I know; some names have been changed, and some are called by their true names. What's important is the lessons we can glean from one another.

As a person of faith, there are times I talk about God, his goodness, and my journey with him along the way. Throughout my life, I've written my thoughts and prayers in journals, and I'll share some of those entries with you as we go along. If you and I don't share a common faith, I still believe that there is enough here to encourage and inspire you, so I hope you'll come along and see what you find. When I do share my faith, I'll do so as authentically as I can, as it's my lived experience. I see and honor yours, too.

I'm also risk averse (hello to all my other first-born children) and someone who battles with the low hum of on-and-off anxiety. I wrote this for others who need a nudge to get out of their own heads, stop overthinking, be brave, and get going. If you're someone for whom being brave and getting going comes easily, then will you connect with me on the socials and tell me how you live your life? I'm always looking for new ideas and inspiration. Will you also share this book with someone in your life with whom you think it might resonate?

Writing my journey into an entire book was a massive exercise in stretching the limits of my risk aversion and getting out of my own head. The guidance I had about writing a first draft was just to write, that editing will come later, and just get your ideas out. So I did that, sent the manuscript to my editor, and began the agonizing wait while she read it. A wait filled with, "Is it good enough?" "Will it capture people's attention and hearts?" "Will they care?"

What came back was a yes to all. It was a Thursday night, and I hung up the phone with my editor from our first conversation after her initial read-through of the manuscript. She affirmed all the things I needed affirmed and had the perfect constructive feedback on exactly the things I thought were too soft as well. I love her, adore her. She is a velvet hammer, soft and smooth in her harshest of critiques. The perfect partner for me in this process.

The last item she gave me was that the opening of the book needs a story. "The reader should be thrust into the middle of your journey so they understand what this is about." *Okay,* I thought. *Agreed, good advice. But all my best stories are in there. I'll need to mine my memory and old Instagram posts for more resources.*

I'll have space to do that on my walk tonight, I thought. *Which will be right after I stop at the neighbor's to get the inside scoop on watching their dog this weekend. Also, I'm hungry, it's dinnertime, and all I had for lunch was carrots and dip. It's fine. I'll get the dog info, walk, then eat. All good.*

A quick drop by the neighbor's turned into two glasses of wine and an hour of snuggling the pup before I started my walk. Feeling both the effects of pounding two generous glasses of California white, as well as a tropical storm from the Gulf of Mexico all the way in the northeast—it was dripping rain—I pulled my hoodie up and headed out for laps around the park that borders my yard.

I started past my own house, creamy light from my kitchen and living room windows shining on the walking trail. I pulled out my phone, opened Instagram, and started to scroll down, down into the recesses—years gone by on the grid of my account. Before I made it to the content I was looking for, a picture reminded me of the month I spent with my niece and nephew, my brother's kids. In a flash, I remembered the night we watched *Moana* at my mom's house, and I knew immediately, that's it. That's the story. I had tried to include the story of that night—and how profound the character of Moana was to me—in the first draft of this book, but I couldn't work it in. So it was cut out, left in a lonely document somewhere, not quite fitting in.

I closed Instagram, opened the music app, and started listening to the soundtrack, specifically: "How Far I'll Go," "We Know the Way," and "I am Moana." If you've not yet seen the movie, those song titles won't mean much to you, but if you have seen it, you'll soon know why I chose those songs.

As I walked the path around the park next to my house, the mix of solitude, dusk, and rain clouds augmented the Polynesian soundtrack in my ears. I was overwhelmed with clarity. The story of Moana had been a mile marker on this fernweh journey for me.

The night I first saw it, simply watching a Disney movie on the couch with my niece and my mom, I realized the story encapsulated everything I learned in my year of travel. Now, four years later, the story of Moana still captures the sense of not just adventure, but the freedom that I felt. I began to cry as I walked. Then sob. I sobbed so loudly that I covered my mouth with my sleeve to muffle the sound. (I mean, I have neighbors after all.) Huge raindrops mixed with my tears as I walked, contemplating the culmination of years pursuing adventure, identity, freedom, mistakes, and joy.

Every time the circular walking path took me past my own house, the warmth of the light from home mixed with the sense of possibility and adventure of the music in my ears. I felt the overwhelming joy of actually doing this thing I had dreamed of my whole life and only recently gave myself permission to pursue.

This girl, this fictional character, understood me and sang songs that gave me words for the depth of emotions in this moment and in many moments along the way. Maybe it was the emotion, or perhaps it was a bit of the Riesling, but I threw my arms in the air in celebration and glee as I walked, dodging puddles while my feet hit the ground to the beat of the island drums. I was home, and I was a voyager, all in the same space.

That, my friends, is what fernweh is about. When you are wholly yourself and yet ever full of change and potential, all at once. Fernweh feels like a dream, an idea out there somewhere. In this time together, we are going to pull it in closer, let it become more tangible. My hope for you is that what feels like an impossible ideation comes into focus, and perhaps even into action, as we walk this road together to discover and follow our unique fernweh.

PART 1

Discover Your Fernweh

CHAPTER ONE

What is Fernweh?

We were three generations of women, snuggling up on the couch on a summer night. All the lights were out, and the magic of Cinderella's castle filled the screen in the opening titles. My mom, my five-year-old niece, and I were having a girls' movie night. Pretty standard stuff for a night at home. Yet, within the first ten minutes of the movie, I was in tears.

My niece, fully in that sweet stage of frilly dresses, painted nails, and Disney princesses, was visiting from Japan for a month. My brother moved to Japan a decade or so before, fell in love, started a family, and now I have a niece and nephew who I adore and see about once a year when they visit the States.

That visit was especially treasured, as I was off work completely, all my worldly possessions packed in my mom's garage and a storage unit. I was counting down the days to when I would move 3,000 miles across the country to start a new life in Boston.

That night on the couch nestled neatly in the middle of four weeks of pool days, tea parties, impromptu dance recitals, board games, s'mores by the backyard fire pit, afternoon bubbles and chalk drawings, and all of us looking forward to our first trip together to Disneyland at the end of the month. We were tan from days in the sun, exhausted from constant play, and deeply connected together from unending and unstructured time as a family.

As *Moana* played on the screen, I tried to disguise the crying, but my niece heard me sniffle and whipped her head toward me. "Are you *crying*?" she questioned, her voice a cute childlike combination of English with a tinge of a Japanese accent. When I confirmed that I was, she wanted to know why. I told her I was crying because I was so happy, because the story was beautiful.

Perhaps you can relate and, like me, shed more tears over happy things than sad ones. I am often overwhelmed by beauty and goodness on film, and I just cry. Once, the first time I went to the movies with a new man friend, I cried over the trailer for an animated film about a girl and her horse. A cartoon trailer. And I was in tears. So, yeah.

To be fair, by the end of *Moana*, we were all in tears. My niece, her auntie (me), and her grammie were all crying over the story of this girl who followed a longing deep inside her, found her purpose, and saved her people. I can't think of anything better to cry about, actually.

Moana, she gets me. She's a gal with big expectations riding on her, laid out for her by family and history. But she just can't get on

board. She goes through the motions, tries to be a good da
but as she walks along the ocean shore each day, dutifully learning to step into her preset responsibilities, the waves call out to
her. And not just the soft foamy waves that tickle her toes, but the
big crashing waves out past the reef—where the water is deep and
dark, the animals are huge and unfamiliar, and the wind is strong
and fierce. That is the place—although she has never been there—
she knows is meant for her.

She also knows that if she doesn't at least try to reach for this
thing that she's never seen, abandon everything she has known,
and put her comfort at risk, she will never be wholly herself. She
will live her whole life and feel as though she just scratched the
surface of who she was made to be.

As I watched this fictional character wrestle with her situation, stumble as she chased her destiny, face fear and uncertainty
at every turn, come to grips with the fact that once you go so far
there is no turning back, and then eventually step fully into who
she was made to be—I began to weep. It was my story. The one I'd
found myself fully immersed in just months prior and that continues to this day.

It was the story of following my fernweh.

In English, we use the word "homesick" to describe the feeling
of being far from home and wishing we could be back there. Merriam-Webster describes homesick as, "longing for home and family while absent from them." The German language has a word for
this, too: *heimweh*. *Heim*, meaning home, and *weh*, meaning grief,
misery, or yearning.

Unlike English, the German language also has a word for the opposite of homesick. Like me, did you just think, *There is an opposite of homesick?* There is, and Germans call it *fernweh* (pronounced fern-veh). *Fern,* meaning distance, and *weh,* meaning grief, misery, or yearning. A yearning for things far away, a longing for distant places.

Germans are well-known travelers and adventurers, so they have also given us a word that you may be more familiar with: *wanderlust.* This one translates to the enjoyment of travel. At first glance, these two may seem like the same word. However, while wanderlust is the enjoyment and most likely fulfillment of travel, fernweh is a deep longing. A heart's ache for far-off places we have never been.

In its purest definition, fernweh is a longing for physical places.

German is not my language, but I understand their word *fernweh.* I feel it deep in my bones. It's like an ancient drumbeat that sometimes is so faint it's hard to even remember and other times is so loud it's all I can focus on.

When I first discovered the word fernweh, I was looking for a way to describe a feeling I'd carried with me my entire life: that there were people yet to meet, streets still to explore, grand vistas to marvel over, and tastes and smells to take in. There had always been an ache, an open space in my soul, a sense that there was something missing. It was like something I'd never encountered before was beckoning from afar.

As I approached the start of my fourth decade, that drumbeat was getting louder. I was restless, unfulfilled, and itchy. Each year had become a routine of similar cycles, events, and dare I say, rhythms. The thing is, those rhythms weren't my drumbeat. I was out of step because it was the wrong beat for my life. But I could hear *my* beat, kind of faint but getting louder, off in the distance.

In response, I rearranged everything in my life, everything I knew, and went all in on finding the source of that sound.

The year I turned forty, I put all of my worldly possessions into storage, rented a room from my family by the week so I had a home base, and set out to explore living in other cities. "A year on the road," I called it. That journey took me to eight countries and six states, plus the District of Colombia. There were dozens of flights and thousands of miles. There were 184 nights away from home: seventy-two in hotels, sixty-seven Airbnb stays, forty nights with friends and family, and five nights on planes.

Along the way, I got my first nephew, first bad hair color, and first crown (dental, not royal). I went crabbing for my dinner on a kayak, was kicked off the stage at Shakespeare's Globe Theatre, saw U2 in concert in a new country, and earned a trip to the ER.

I had a lot of great dates and turned down a lot more. Found love and lost it again. Had more time with my parents than I'd ever had in my adult life. Reconnected with old friends, made countless new ones, and worked to keep the rest close even with the distance. I lost one friend to brokenness and surrendered another to heaven. I spent the first half of the year doing a lot of talking and the second half learning to listen more.

At the end of it all, I found that everything I need fits into one suitcase and a carry-on, with room for treasures to bring home. I took a huge leap forward into becoming the woman I'd always dreamed I wanted to be. I was assured that the God of heaven and earth loves us and is with us every step. And along the way, I discovered that each of us, just regular people living our lives, have a longing deep within us that calls us to follow it.

Fernweh calls to us from deep inside our souls. It is something that, if we live our whole lifetime and let it go unanswered, we will somehow have missed out on the "big thing." You may feel a sense of it right now. Your heart might be fluttering like faint butterfly wings as you learn about the idea of fernweh. Or your heart may start to race in your chest as you recognize a longing from deep within.

Either way, your fernweh is there. It's the thing that you imagined for yourself, but didn't have the strength, knowledge, resources, or hope enough to go after. It's the thing you've seen someone else do and told yourself that you could never do that. It's the thing you stopped in its tracks before the disappointment could hop over the back fence into your life and overwhelm you. That. That thing right there is your fernweh.

But wait, fernweh is the longing for places, no? Yes, in its true linguistic translation, it means physical places. I believe we can stretch that definition to include the things in our life left undiscovered. For me, my fernweh was far-off geographical destinations. Yet, I know people who have always lived in the same country, or even city, who are chasing their fernweh. I know people who were pursued by their fernweh for ten years until they finally went back to school, started that business, or wrote that book.

I have this friend, Beth, who is an achiever and a great student. She finished her undergrad and then went on to respiratory therapy school, eventually working in a hospital. She got married to her high school love, after a few years of them exploring the world independently of one another. Ezra, her husband, is one of the greatest humans you could ever meet. They moved to the Pacific Northwest, had a sweet girl, bought a house, and got some chickens and an abundance of houseplants.

Somewhere in that rainy climate, Beth discovered pottery. It started as a creative outlet for her. Slowly, it became something she shared with friends, as gifts, and she posted a few pics on social media. Then more folks who saw her pieces wanted their own. So she stepped into that world, creating a website and giving her studio a name, Cactus and Clay Ceramics. I was honored to see a preview of the website before she launched it, in part so I could buy two cups she'd made. I was her first customer, and probably a bit bothersome about when the site would be done so I could buy the cups I'd seen on Instagram. Because they were gorgeous and because, Get after it, lady!

On her website, Beth tells her story like this:

Pottery is what I do for me. It fills my cup. It is my therapy.

It is my sincere hope that each piece I create is used and loved in your home. I hope they are on your tables for family dinners, and in your hands for all the ups and downs that life throws your way. I hope they become heirlooms that you pass on to your children and your children's children.

I am honored and humbled that you let me into your lives this way.

Beth's aesthetic shows in her art, and her values show in her business. She uses sustainable materials and practices in her pieces and packaging, and she donates a portion of the proceeds to a local organization supporting at-risk and homeless youth.

Since starting Cactus and Clay, she's connected with other female small business owners, promoting collaboration and encouraging consumers to support entrepreneurship. Beth is an introvert who does this all from her home. She didn't intend it to land where it has and may have no idea where her creativity will take her next. She found something she was passionate about, that filled her bucket, and she found a way to share it with others. Beth told me, "I firmly believe that when you pursue the thing you are passionate about, it's amazing the opportunities that come your way." She is following her fernweh, and it's changing her life. All from her garage.

For some, fernweh is a lofty goal, or something that's never been done before. As the future of space travel changes rapidly, moving from a government-organized endeavor to a commercially available experience, one of the engineers of a highly anticipated and publicized flight said, "We've taken the impossible and we're making it inevitable." To have some of that confidence, *amiright*?

For others, fernweh is in the arts, business, career, or hobbies. I've known folks whose fernweh calling has to do with fitness, dogs, building a family, their community, or nonprofit work. Sometimes it's travel, cooking, education, or health. There is no measure of value on someone's fernweh; it is their own passion to pursue what God wired inside them to love. It can be anything.

What fernweh is, and how it shows up for you, is personal. But it is almost always far away from where you are now. Fernweh is an adventure of distance and uncertainty. It is often audaciously big, and does not make sense, at first, to other people around you. But it will make sense to you; it will make sense in the core of who you are.

So, let's explore fernweh together. Along the way, I'll tell you all about my year of travel, and some other people's fernweh stories, too. And as we continue our conversation through these pages, let's exude understanding for both ourselves and for others. Let's recognize that others are learning to discover their fernweh and give them space to do just that. Let's also give ourselves the space to discover and explore our own fernweh, as well.

You may have no idea what path to take, what to pack, or how to prepare. And that doesn't matter just now because you simply know you have a fernweh calling and you want to pursue it. Whatever "it" is. You want to see what is down that road, even if just for the joy of the journey. Even if you fail or turn back, the pursuit to find out where that drumbeat is coming from will be worth it.

Every good journey starts with discovery, and so you'll spend the next several chapters learning to recognize what fernweh looks like in your own life. How does it reveal itself? Where does it come from? Is it really there, even if you can't feel it? I propose that yes, it is, and it's been there all along. Your fernweh is part of you. It's simply waiting for you to see it, hear it, and respond.

So what do you think—are you ready to follow your fernweh?

In this next chapter, there will be mention of suicidal ideation. Please know that while my personal experience with these thoughts didn't last very long, I understand this is not the experience for everyone. Do what is necessary to care for yourself, including skipping ahead to the following chapter.

CHAPTER TWO

Your Fernweh is a Drumbeat

You know how sometimes everything in your life seems to line up in the right place, at the right time? All the puzzle pieces fitting together to make something beautiful—with a precision that can only be attributed to a Creator and Maker of all things?

A few months before I turned forty, that gorgeous convergence of timing and logistics was obscenely far away. In fact, it seemed as if all things were beginning to unfold in a series of events headed into a vacuum, a black hole of loneliness and being alone. Not only that, but somewhere along the way I had lost track of the drumbeat that had previously called to me so clearly.

For fifteen years, I'd called San Jose, in Silicon Valley, California, my home. Every few years, I flirted with the idea of moving to a new city, finding a new job, and making a new start. But San

Jose was home. Home enough. Friendships I had developed over a decade transformed into family as we shared life and adventures together. But as I closed in on my fortieth birthday, it hit me that I'd been hanging around helping everyone else live the life I'd dreamed of. I longed for a partner, to build a home together, perhaps start a family, but it never came. I was intentional about my dating life, mindful to not fall head over heels for someone who didn't fit the life I wanted, hoping to find someone to share my faith, and I was alone a lot. Alone when I was actually alone, and alone, also, in social situations.

A lot of my social time, especially as a church gal, was spent with married folks. There was a lot of time spent with just girlfriends, amazing women who always encouraged me in my life and valued me deeply for who I was. However, it was unavoidable that we would talk about how life was going, how it changed and moved forward. They all had weddings, in-laws, buying houses, the stages of having kids to talk about. I hadn't experienced any of that personally, so I learned to speak fluent "married mom," although I'd never been one. It was a language to which I could easily code-switch.

During this time in my life, I joined married friends and their kids on adventures, melting into the fifth seat in the car, taking that end spot at the dinner table, working friend hangouts around naps and after-school schedules. As time passed, a first birthday party had suddenly become the tenth one. I was starting to get a feeling deep in my soul that this wasn't my lane. That while I loved my people so, so deeply, I was trying too hard to travel in tandem with them on a journey that wasn't mine. I wasn't figuring out newlywed communication, or sleep training, and I had no one to take to gymnastics or swim lessons. And yet there was a lot of time and space in my own life that I'd left undiscovered as I chose community over myself.

Then, in a matter of just a few months, everything changed. Four of my five closest friends all announced they were moving away. One, just over an hour drive, and the farthest, to another hemisphere. But that was just the beginning.

Next, my landlord announced she would be selling our house, which meant saying a premature goodbye to my roommates. One would be married within a few months; the others decided it was time to move closer to their jobs, in a direction much farther from mine.

After a decade and a half of investing my life in a place, in the people of that place, and in growing myself as a person, the dock ties were being loosed. Things were starting to pull away, to bang against what had always been, to sail for the next shore. But all I felt were the waves, the beating, the motion sickness. Loneliness, hopelessness, and darkness existed where a future should have been. I was without home and without community. I was about to turn forty. I began to wonder a lot, *Is this all that life holds for me?*

I didn't know what to do, so I pulled out my journal and began to write my prayers:

May 2nd

I'm lonely, God.

I want to know that my life matters. That I have a purpose. And right now I feel like I could step out and no one would care. That people would be sad for a second that I'm gone, but there would be no ache that something is missing. That, in fact, there would be a relief.

If I were gone, that hole in the ground would be filled in and never thought of again. I see myself as having no value, and my circumstances reinforce that.

I felt hopeless, purposeless. It felt like this huge milestone birthday loomed in front of me like the edge of a cliff, and each day that went by pushed me closer and closer to falling over the edge of it into an abyss of the same repetitive cycle, year after year, for the next forty years.

The house I shared with my friends, the one I was leaving, sat right next to the train tracks. When I say right, I mean *right*. We could make eye contact with commuters from our kitchen table. All day and all night—commuter trains, Amtrak, freight trains, the sound of the crossing gate warning, the headlights and rumble of the heavy rail. And that horn. It still rings in my head and makes my teeth hurt.

There were two instances, however, when the sound of that horn called to me. Like a siren calling the sailors in Homer's *Odyssey*, that horn tried to lure me out of my loneliness and desperation and into the night. I imagined what it would feel like to sit on those tracks, clutching my knees, seeing just a headlight, brighter and brighter. With each second of heavy rail rumble, that horn would tell me to move, to get off the tracks. I wasn't sure if I would.

That was it. Just two times did those self-harming thoughts come around. The good news is that the promises of God came flooding back to my mind louder than that horn, quicker and clearer in their intent than the voice of hopelessness. Promises not to harm me, but to give me a future full of hope. That sound drowned out all others, no matter how faint it called in the beginning.

In that same journal entry, where I'd found myself at the bottom of an empty well of loneliness and hopelessness, I prayed to God:

Right now I feel like I'm on the outside looking in, but I want to be part of this wonderful world you have created. I'm sitting in my room hearing birds chirp and seeing the sunshine on a beautiful morning, and I want to live and thrive and change the world.

I can't do that where I am. Is this you severing my ties to my current life so I can go in pursuit of the next one? I keep seeing myself being on the road next year. A year on the road, to explore. These feelings of not belonging, is it because you want me to move on?

That has more hope and answers than staying here and being swallowed by a black hole of loneliness. And to tell my story. That seems more real and true than anything else.

In what seemed like a moment, a very distinct dream began to take shape. I experienced flashes of clarity in the bottom of that darkness. I thought, if I am not actually in the same stage of life as the people in my community, if I haven't yet been given the gifts they have, then what *have* I been given?

In her book, *It's Not Your Turn: What to Do While You're Waiting for Your Breakthrough*, Heather Thompson Day says, "The best thing that happened to my faith was watching other people open packages I had ordered." I think it was similar for me. Watching other people live the dreams I thought were mine, and having my table setting stay empty, brought me to a place of serious introspection and conversations with God.

These conversations meant realigning with the adventure God had made for me, the adventure I was currently missing because I was looking at other people's gifts. It was time to stop asking what I was missing and start asking what I'd been gifted that perhaps others hadn't. I had to start asking myself—right where I am, and with what I have, how big and loud can this life get? That single question changed everything. Have you ever asked it of yourself? It's a powerful one, so be ready when you do.

A year on the road, to explore. In my spirit, I knew change was coming. The drumbeat of that idea was calling—faint, but getting stronger. My fortieth birthday was in September, and nine months earlier, long before the lowest thoughts crept in, I'd written this prayer in my journal:

January 3rd

This morning I reread my goals for this year and realized that while they are functional, I am not passionate about them. There is not a big enough risk and big enough faith. I am not excited about them.

I need to dream bigger this year. And redo my goals. And quit calling them goals, but call them dreams, and I will watch you answer them. And make them come true. That seems like a lot more fun!

This was months before the news of friends moving away, months before the train tracks, and months before I began to ask the big "what if" questions. God was illuminating a part of my desires and my destiny that I'd tucked into the attic and allowed to be covered in dust. This first journal entry of that year was the breaking of the seal on the destiny treasure map. *I need to dream bigger this year.* Daring to crack it open and see what dangers and rewards might be revealed.

A few days later, a little more of the map was unrolled, as I started my journal entry for the day with my Bible verse for the year, a passage from Ephesians:

Now to him who is able to do far more abundantly than all that we ask or think according to the power at work within us.

Ephesians 3:20

I dug into the meaning of the verse even more, and looked up the word "abundant," which means richly supplied, overflowing fullness. Then I opened the reading from a book of daily faith-based readings, *Jesus Calling*, and Ephesians 3:20 just happened to be the Bible verse of the day there, too. Mind you, I wrote the verse in my journal first, then found it in the daily reading. God works in my life a lot that way. It was weird for a while, but now I've come to expect it. It's still fun every time, just not so odd anymore. So the daily reading said, "There is no limit to what I can accomplish!" and I wrote my prayers in my journal that day:

January 6th

A friend said recently that you would reveal things to me through dreams, and that this is the year to go big. I want to believe this, God. Help me to see what you see. Help my heart and mind to dream of the things of you and what your heart dreams for this world and its people. Thank you, God. Thank you for a renewed vision for the year.

There is a saying that people only change when the pain of staying the same outweighs the pain of changing. Does that mean you must first come to a breaking point before you can discover your fernweh? No, no, of course not. Though for me personally, I did. I had a tipping point.

Think of the people in your life who have made a big change and chased something audacious. I would venture to say they fall into a couple of categories. They are someone who has finally come to a place where staying the same is worse than moving in a new direction, worse than even possibly failing. Or they are someone who has already been through that cycle before and now knows that it's not worth wasting their time overthinking it. They have risked big once and know that it's not as scary as it seemed.

For me, it took that season of life to realize that something was missing. Something that used to call to me, a longing to travel and explore, had been dormant for far too long. While I didn't yet have the word fernweh to clarify what I was feeling, I could sense the return of a drumbeat from my childhood and my former years. I could hear it, ever faintly, and I began to look around for its source and wonder how I might follow it.

But before we move on to what came next for me, let's talk about you. This is such a pivotal part of the fernweh journey, because it is the moment we acknowledge the ache or longing in our lives. What is happening in your heart and in your spirit right now? Truly. If you need to take a second for yourself, then set this book down and have a moment with your own dreams.

Is there something that used to call to you, and it's become dormant?

Is there something stirring in your soul and spirit right now?

If you are someone who talks to and trusts God, ask him to show you a drumbeat that has been in your heart all along, but has become faint. Ask him to make it beat louder.

Does something specific come to mind? Write it down somewhere. Here in this book is fine, or in a journal. In the notes on your phone. You don't have to do anything with it just yet. Hear it call to you, however far away it is. Faint is okay; just listen for that sound.

CHAPTER THREE

Trail Markers Point the Way

More than a few people have asked me how I got such a voracious desire to travel. I've lived in seven states across the U.S.—in almost every time zone—from Hawaii to Massachusetts. I've traveled much around Western Europe, been to Asia multiple times, and had a couple short stints living in Latin America. Even with all that, I feel like I've barely seen much of this world.

At one point, I got myself one of those scratch-off world maps, the kind where the country is covered in gold foil and after you visit, you scratch off the foil to reveal the country underneath. The day it arrived, I gleefully got out a quarter and began to scratch away states and countries, remembering the incredible adventures along the way. About ten minutes later, I was done scratching, stood back, and saw almost an entire sheet of gold staring back at me. That map was calling me out. There were still so many more places to go.

The funny thing is my brother has a similar need to see the world. Maybe even more than I do. In his late twenties, he moved to Japan for two years to teach English, came home to California for less than a year, and left again for two and half years to join the Peace Corps in Zambia, a country in the southern part of central Africa. When he returned from Zambia, he regrouped his life, looked for jobs in Japan, and got back there as quickly as he could.

Like a lot of fernweh journeys, you could probably trace yours back to early experiences, family interests, and environment. I can see parallels in a lot of people's fernweh journeys—experiences they had as children, things their family did together, family heritage, and history brought forward—swirled together to form their fernweh. I also recognize this isn't always the case. Sometimes we want to go far away from how we were raised, but looking back can also help us identify our fernweh and recognize that it may have been around in our lives for a while. The threads from our experiences and history are like trail markers, guiding us toward a destination, toward our fernweh.

My brother and I share the desire to go and find new and faraway places. But why can't we just be content to live in the small town we grew up in, stay near our parents, and have Sunday dinner get-togethers? A look at the trail markers of our lives provides a pretty clear picture.

We grew up in a small coastal, agricultural community almost directly centered between two of America's largest cities, Los Angeles and San Francisco. What we lacked in big-city resources, we made up for in lemonade stands and going home when the streetlights came on. But when we did need something a big city offered—like a prom dress, a medical specialist, a sporting event or concert—we traveled.

With grandparents to both the north and the south of us, a family skiing habit, an active youth group, and a kid (my brother) who played competitive sports, my family, in particular, was on the move a lot. We traveled up and down the state, and were experts in packing the car for road trips. I always sensed there was more out there to see. Every road trip to Los Angeles included hours of driving in view of the Pacific Ocean. That alone will cause someone to wonder what lies beyond the horizon.

I knew when I was still quite young that there just had to be more than what I could see in front of me. I felt it deep in my soul, in my spirit.

Our active lifestyle wasn't the only influence on my desire to "go." We lived in a cute little house with no dining room to speak of, so our dining table was in a pass-through space, pushed up against the wall. My seat was on the long side, facing the wall, and above the table hung a topographical map of the United States. It was the kind where the mountains bumped out, and the land changed color depending on the type of terrain. The plains were yellow, rivers were blue, and mountains were green or sometimes snowcapped white on top if they were especially tall.

Not only did that map hang there above our dinner each night, but we talked about it as a regular part of our mealtime conversations. Our parents told us of the places they had visited, the people they knew around the country, and where we would next visit together as a family of four. My dad studied science in his undergrad education, so he talked of the geology of different places and the history of the U.S. land migration. That map was a magical place of learning, family, adventure, and dreams. Yet another trail marker.

Not only did we *talk* about getting out there and seeing new places, but my parents had the experience to prove it was more than just theory. When they were first married, my dad finished his degree in biology and took a job in the middle of Los Angeles doing cancer research. He was working in a basement lab with no windows, commuting in L.A. traffic, and my parents felt stuck just as they started their life together. So they planned and budgeted and quit that life.

They packed up their orange Ford Econoline van, outfitted for camping, a big homemade gear box on the roof, and set off across the country with their black Labrador retriever and $1,200. They were gone for three months, camping, fishing, hiking, and sightseeing. They planned their route to visit friends along the way: northern route on the way to the East Coast, southern route back.

Their cross-country trip and my childhood happened in the days of film cameras, when people turned the negatives into slides. (If you have no idea what those words mean, google them.) When we were kids, every so often on a weekend night after dinner, my parents would load up the slide projector, turn off the lights in the house, and tell us the story of their grand road trip adventure. To the soundtrack of the projector fan whirring and the click of advancing slides, I saw my mom's 1970s headscarf and high-waist-ed pants and my dad's lamb chop sideburns appear in sepia tone in front of places I couldn't have imagined existed. I never got enough of hearing about that trip, the fun they had, and the people they saw along the way. It fueled a far-off call in my heart, one that only got louder as I got older.

There is a moment in the story of Moana when she is about to give up the call of the ocean and settle into her dutiful role as the next village chief. Her grandmother, Gramma Tala, takes her to the entrance of a secret cave, pulls back the vines, and sends her in. There, Moana finds that while her father has been telling her that their island is the best place to be, the place they were meant to stay, her ancestors actually lived on boats, sailing across the ocean to find new islands. When it was time for them to chart a new course and find a new island, they pushed off from the shore and sailed again.

Moana comes running out of the cave, flailing her arms about and screaming, "We were voyagers! WE WERE VOYAGERS!" What she uncovered in that cave was that the feeling brewing inside her was not a fleeting thought or a crazy idea. It came from generations back in her heritage. It was her destiny.

My great grandparents left Ireland in the early 1900s with a few trunks of their most precious possessions and a baby, coming through Ellis Island on their way to the West Coast. Their son became ill and passed away shortly after they made it to California, and they never set foot in their home country again. They found a new home, a new community, and started a legacy that was passed down to me.

When you think about your own fernweh—what it is or what it could possibly be—is there family folklore that stirs your heart or ignites a passion in you? Perhaps your family tells tales of artists, achievement, discovery, or home. When you look back through your family tree, it's quite possible that there are fernweh dots to be connected through a cast of characters who walked through this life before you.

I've always been fiercely independent and strong willed. Growing up, I heard "bossy" more than once in reference to my leadership style. By now, we all know from Sheryl Sandberg's book, *Lean In*, that we do not call a woman bossy, but instead call out her strong leadership qualities. Perhaps it's best said by Beyoncé, "I'm not bossy. I'm the boss."

My grandmother, on the other side of our family, was also fiercely independent and strong willed. She was one of the best shots at the rifle range, and she rode motorcycles as a single gal and even after she was married. When I say she rode them, I don't mean as the passenger. She was the driver, in full leathers and dark sunglasses. And all of this as a woman in the 1930s. She was truly badass. She was also made a widow and a single mother to a young son when her first husband was killed in a motorcycle accident. She had to provide for her child and make her way in a world that was not ready for women like her.

My heritage is dotted with travelers and independent thinkers, mavericks who paved a new path. It was always there for me; I just had to uncover it and give myself permission to embrace it.

When you think about your family tree and folklore, is there a common thread that winds through the generations? Is it a career path, a skill, or a character trait? Pause a moment, if you like, and write out your family tree. Think about what you know about the experiences and personalities of each generation. If you don't know much of your family backstory, find someone in your family who does and ask them about it. Perhaps they will, like Moana's grandmother, pull back a curtain to reveal a past you didn't know existed.

Uncovering your fernweh is not just about family heritage, but about reflecting on your lived experience, too. In *Moana*, there is a character named Maui who starts as an adversary of Moana's, but soon becomes a friend to our heroine. Maui is a seasoned voyager, sailing a boat with ease and reading the stars like the best navigation app. He uses his hands, the water temperature, the wind, and other markers to plan which direction to turn, and he is confident in his calculations and decisions. Moana asks him about what he's doing, and he says, "It's called *wayfinding*. It's seeing where you're going in your mind, knowing where you are by knowing where you've been."

One summer, in elementary school, my parents took my brother and me on our own grand road trip, driving up the West Coast from California to Vancouver, Canada, and back. We loaded up our wood-paneled station wagon, my mom making "nests" in the back seat for us out of blankets and pillows, and we set out for two weeks on a journey far from home to undiscovered lands like Oregon and Washington.

We embraced everything we saw along the way. My dad, ever a scientist and teacher, pointed out history, biology, ecology, and anthropology on every stretch of road. We went rafting in a river in a whole different state, we climbed under the streets of Seattle to see sidewalks and storefronts long forgotten after a flood, we drove our car onto a boat to be ferried into an entirely different country, and we were enveloped in the magic of the Sunken Garden at Butchart Gardens. We unfolded and folded the highlighted AAA paper maps a million times as we found our way.

I was allowed one special souvenir from that trip, so I carefully watched the gift shop selections at each new place we visited, waiting for the right thing that would help me remember this adventure. It was at the end of one of our days in Canada when I found it. A small oval pewter box, about an inch and a half around. The box was mostly gray, and on the lid was the image of a unicorn in a garden with a rainbow in full color in the background. Two of the flowers were actually earrings, and upon opening the box, I discovered the lid was a brooch that could be worn, and inside the box was a necklace with a pewter unicorn charm. Could anything be more magical for a seven-year-old girl?

That unicorn box has a place of honor in my jewelry collection even today. Close to four decades later, seeing it still stirs in me the feeling of freedom and adventure I was introduced to on my first grand road trip. Those two weeks felt like a lifetime and became a trail marker in my life.

It feels important to remind you in this moment about the true meaning of fernweh as we talk about it in this context. Much of what I share about my personal story has to do with travel, and you'll remember that the literal definition of fernweh alludes to actual physical places.

We've expanded the definition of fernweh to include any adventure or dream that feels distant. It is not just a longing for far-off physical places, but a longing for adventure. Yet, our culture has somehow come to define adventure as travel.

However, Dictionary.com describes adventure this way: "an exciting or very unusual experience," "~participation in exciting undertakings or enterprises."

Merriam-Webster defines adventure as "an exciting or remarkable experience."

If we broaden our definition and let go of the idea that fernweh is about travel adventure, we can begin to see how an exciting or remarkable experience—that thing that fuels our fire—*is* our adventure. Discovering what that is starts with exploring your history and your experiences. These are the trail markers that help you *wayfind*—knowing where you're going based on where you are and where you've been.

When you look back on where you've been, do you have experiences and trail markers that come to mind? That is your fernweh. Whatever that is for you, it's time to bring it into focus.

CHAPTER FOUR

It Doesn't Always Make Sense

A fun fact about me is that I speak Spanish. I actually have a degree in Spanish from university, and while my verb conjugation still needs work, my accent is pretty on point for a non-native speaker. On my very first day of Spanish class in ninth grade, we learned a few basic nouns, adjectives, and articles. I came home from school that day repeating the phrase we'd learned, "la muchacha bonita," *the beautiful girl*, and felt like I'd discovered a new universe. It was as if I was peering through a portal into ideas that had always been there, in tandem with my world, but I'd had no sense of their presence for all my fourteen years so far. With three little words, my world exploded into a galaxy of possibility.

Learning Spanish, and the doors it opened, was irresistible. I couldn't stay away from languages, so much so that when I'd finished the required two years of language for graduation, I did another two with Spanish and added a year of German. Admittedly, I'm a linguaphile, but loving and learning languages isn't just about the words. Tied up in language is culture, history, social constructs, and outside influences. Learning another language, even while in your own country, is a journey to new places all on its own.

Those three little words I learned that day in ninth grade evolved into service trips to Mexico, a summer building homes in Tijuana, a month in Guatemala for language school, a bachelor's degree in Spanish, open hearts and minds from strangers, lots of extra sides of guacamole, and overflowing splashes of tequila in my margaritas. Oh, and also some really legit cross-cultural flirting.

I had an immediate love of learning a new language and kept pursuing it with every new opportunity that came. Did I have a definitive end goal in mind? Not really. It just made me happy; it made sense to me. I didn't really ask, *To what end am I doing this*? It didn't matter. Learning Spanish was creative and life-giving, and that was enough in the moment.

That's the thing about fernweh. It doesn't really have to make sense; it just is. The simple *pursuit* of it can be enough. Now, does that mean if your fernweh is to start a nonprofit or complete a PhD, you're taking it too far? No way. Fernweh can absolutely include specific and tangible goals. The thing that makes it *your* fernweh is that the call to pursue it comes from deep within *you*, first and foremost. That is enough; it's often all you need. Where it takes you, however, might be endless.

In college, I spent a summer living in Tijuana, Mexico, working as a volunteer intern for an organization called Amor Ministries. Amor bridges the service of religious and community volunteer groups with the need for housing in the poorest areas around the U.S./Mexico border. My role was to be at the site of a new home being constructed for a local family, show the volunteers how to assemble the house from the foundation footers to the roof, offer translation help, and be a connection between the organization, the volunteers, the family receiving the home, and the local church.

I was nineteen years old, sleeping on a cot in a giant army tent, and using pit toilets and bucket showers. It was, even to this day, one of the greatest summers of my life.

On the way to Mexico, our team of new interns from across the country came together for a few days in Los Angeles for orientation and team building. There were lessons on the history of the organization and their connection to the community, as well as training in communication and cultural awareness and adaptation. One of the most valuable lessons from those first few days was a simple one I've carried with me throughout my life. The easiest and most impactful way to adapt to a culture is to wait, watch, and do as you see.

One of our instructors told a story of how he went to hail a taxi in an Asian country. He stepped to the curb on a bustling city street, put his hand in the air, and waved it about just like he would have hailed a cab in America. No cabs stopped. He watched taxis pull to the curb for pedestrian after pedestrian around him, seemingly without them doing a thing. He wondered, *How on*

earth do the drivers know to stop for these people when they aren't
doing anything to signal that they need a pickup?

So he stopped taking action and stood back to observe. It took him a few minutes of watching to see the subtlety of how locals actually caught a cab. What he saw is that they stepped to the edge of the road, made direct eye contact with a taxi driver, who made eye contact in return, and pulled over to the curb next to them. This might happen from very close by, or across several lanes of traffic, but it was the custom. So he fought the urge to hail a cab with his hand à la the American way and instead set his gaze on a taxi driver's face coming down the road. He did not break his glance and in a matter of moments, found a passenger door lined up square in front of him at the curb, and off he went.

That is a story and a lesson I heard over twenty-five years ago, and it is still fresh in my mind. Like learning those three little Spanish words in the ninth grade, that simple taxi story helped me to see that we can unlock worlds when we observe, step outside of ourselves and off our well-known paths, and try something that we may fail at the first time. But what if we don't fail? What if, instead, we learn that the familiar way we have always known isn't always the best option for the situation? That there are actually many ways to accomplish the same goal? What if we change the goal altogether?

That little story of hailing a cab set a framework for how I approached culture and unpacked my own learning. It helped me to embrace, early on, a mindset of trying things and failing forward. Did it resolve all my insecurities and cause me to be fearless? Well, no. Did it teach me everything I needed to know about cross-cultural communication? (Shakes head.) But it turned the rudder just a smidge, enough to reset the course of how I thought about cultural adventure.

I love how lessons about culture and communication help us in all aspects of our lives. I'm a huge nerd for these things; they make me happy. That is part of how I know that travel, languages, and culture are my fernweh. I could learn about them and try out those learnings endlessly. I will never have enough of these aspects of life, even until the day I leave this earth. I have a feeling there is something that has a similar effect on your life. There's a good chance that's your fernweh.

Once we finished the orientation and got to Mexico, that summer took on a life of its own. Time seemed to stand still as we lived in this magical place of adventure, sun, and purpose. Yes, we had places to be at certain times, but if a car broke down, the neighborhood kids wanted to jump rope in the street, or we had to go on a hunt for a box of nails, it was all part of the adventure in a place outside of real life. Almost like stepping through a wardrobe into a mystical land, except we lived in army tents with no running water or electricity for ten weeks.

My regular outfit each day was overalls, work boots, a huge straw hat, hammer hanging off the side loop at my hip, and a carpenter's pencil stuck in the front pocket. I had blisters, loose nails in my pockets, ate peanut butter and jelly sandwiches almost every single day for lunch, and came home at the end of August with a short-sleeve tan line that rivaled the best Midwestern farmer's tan. And I was blissfully, ecstatically, almost obnoxiously happy.

Friends who hadn't seen me since the spring commented on a massive shift in my confidence and countenance. They had never seen me like this, in my place of full purpose and passion.

The summer I spent in Mexico was intended to be one of service to a community in need, and for sure, it was. What I didn't know at the time was that God was dialing up the volume on that drumbeat that had been calling to me since I was little, staring at the map on the wall and watching the miles pass from the back seat of our station wagon. He was teaching me to hear it, to recognize it, and to dance in time with it. That was the first time I would experience the absolute freedom that comes with moving in the space of exactly where I was designed to be. Over the next two decades, the volume of that drumbeat would ebb and flow, but it would not reach the same level of freedom and joy I had known in Mexico until after I experienced the crisis of confidence and purpose right before turning forty.

I once heard someone say, "I hope everyone has moments that are so special and so personal that they are hard to explain to somebody else."

You truly know you've found your fernweh when your experience of it is enough. You enjoy the process, or at least aspects of it. You see how it's changing you. You see the Creator's hand in it, even if you have not come to the destination yet.

There have been so many moments along my fernweh journey that would be cheapened if I attempted to explain them out loud to another human. There were experiences where, in the moment, I recognized a picture would never come close to capturing what

I was seeing with my eyes, experiencing with my senses, nor how I was feeling in my soul. In those moments, I would often inhale deeply, close my eyes, look around again, and soak in the absolute bliss of being fully present. Many times, I would thank God for having me in that place and time exactly in that moment, awed by his goodness and generosity.

These blissful moments won't mean there will never be hardship, heartbreak, challenges, or monotony. It also won't mean that your fernweh will always make sense. But there exists a satisfaction in the process of following your fernweh that is unlike other pursuits we attempt.

When you are immersed in experiencing your fernweh at full volume, you often don't notice or care where you are or what's around you. Hours pass by. You ignore your phone. You look up and it's dark outside, or you are hungry, and didn't even realize it. All because everything in your spirit is enraptured and filled with purpose and passion. There is nowhere else you would rather be. That's what I got a taste of in Mexico. That's what we are going after on this journey together.

What is it in your life that completely envelops you? That doesn't completely make sense, but it calls to you? Your answer to this question will point you to your fernweh.

CHAPTER FIVE

You're Willing to Fail

We've all seen the memes with some type of message like "failure is not an option." While the sentiment is a good one, conjuring up images of persistence, dedication, and resilience, I would like to push back a bit. Failure is actually a great teacher. If we reject failure as an option, then we may try to power through lessons that could be incredible refining tools, or we might never get started. If we see the act of failing as unacceptable, then we will be paralyzed and unable to begin in the first place.

Friends, failure is part of the process. Trying, swinging, missing, repositioning, and going again is what makes the journey an upward spiral of growth and adventure. Any great story has at least one tension point where the hero (or she-ro) feels as though all hope is lost. It is not the seeming lack of hope that derails a success; it is when we allow that idea to seep into our mind and our soul so much that it grounds us from taking off.

This is where we must connect back to faith, to the reason why we began to pursue the fernweh journey in the first place. In my faith tradition, the scripture in the Bible says, in Paul's letter to the Hebrews: "Now faith is the assurance of what we hope for and the certainty of what we do not see" (Hebrews 11:1).

What if what we hope for and do not yet see isn't a specific outcome or destination, but a promise for the journey itself? A promise that we will be changed at the end of it all, and that we will grow into the person we were made to be. That we will grow in confidence, assurance, faith, and trust. Having hope for the journey itself takes the power away from failure. It makes the outcome of failing or not failing irrelevant because, in the process, we are becoming who we are meant to be.

I see so many places in scripture where God affirms that our purpose is to know him more, over a lifetime of progression toward understanding and becoming like him. In 2 Corinthians, Paul writes to the local church in Corinth, saying, "And we all, who with unveiled faces contemplate the Lord's glory, are being transformed into his image with ever-increasing glory, which comes from the Lord, who is the Spirit" (3:18). Ever-increasing glory. What a phrase. It doesn't mean that we arrive anywhere, but that we are on a lifetime journey of transformation.

In a different letter, this one to the church at Philippi, Paul wrote, "Not that I have already obtained this or am already perfect, but I press on to make it my own, because Christ Jesus has made me his own" (Philippians 3:12). We press on, we dream big, and we allow these experiences to transform us. If this talk of faith doesn't resonate with your belief system, perhaps I can say it like this: our biggest growth as people often comes when we risk and we go after stretching goals, knowing that the win is not a particular outcome, but the fact that we attempted the adventure at all.

I mentioned earlier about my brother, Devin's, time in the Peace Corps. When he left, I was incredibly anxious about him being in such a remote area halfway across the world. He would be living in a hut, hours from a city, with no electricity, running water, or healthcare of any kind. When he arrived in Zambia, he met his team of fellow Americans from all over the United States, including a young man about his age named Wyatt from South Dakota. Wyatt instantly became the life of the group, a natural leader full of mischievous humor, height, athleticism, and affable charm. Everyone who met Wyatt loved him, and his fellow Peace Corps volunteers, including my brother, were no exception.

Before each of the volunteers left for the communities that would be their homes for the next two years, they spent ten weeks training on the specifics of the projects they would run: fish farming and local entrepreneurship. They spent part of their days in the mud at the fishponds and part of their days learning the language of the area of Zambia in which they would each live. They were set to be commissioned as official Peace Corps volunteers in a ceremony that would be televised on Zambia's national TV station.

Wyatt had learned the language of his community so well that he would be giving a speech as part of the program to be broadcast across the country. The night before the ceremony, however, there was an accident, and Wyatt was killed. The details don't matter and, out of respect for him and those close to him, won't be shared. What does matter is the impact this brought to his teammates, forever changing them as individuals and bonding them together as a group.

Fast-forward fifteen years. The anniversary of Wyatt's death was approaching. As a way to honor his friend through a connection to Wyatt's athleticism and zest for life, Devin promised himself he would complete an Ironman triathlon and dedicate his race to Wyatt. If you've not heard of this craziness, an Ironman triathlon is a three-part event consisting of a 2.4-mile swim, 112-mile bike ride, and then running a full marathon of 26.2 miles. The average competitor does it in just under thirteen hours and is supported along the course with water stations, medical tents, and sometimes even massage stations for cramping muscles. Devin signed up for two Ironman events that year with the intent to both honor his friend and attempt to qualify for the granddaddy of all, the Ironman race in Kona, Hawaii.

That was also the year almost every event and group gathering was canceled as a result of a global pandemic, including sporting events and competitions. Devin was feeling the pain of a missed opportunity to remember his friend, but rather than getting stuck in that disappointment, he decided to get creative. One day that spring, he invited a number of us to join a Facebook event called the "Wyatt Memorial Double Ironman Distance Challenge." In the description, he wrote:

Wyatt passed away 15 years ago this fall serving in the United States Peace Corps in Zambia. He was relentless, fearless, and loved a physical challenge. Celebrate his life with me and take on the challenge virtually. Do one part, go for a run of any distance, take a walk, or just spend time alone thinking about Wyatt.

Right about now you might be having the same thought that we all did, which is, *What in the world is a double Ironman?* Well, it is what you think it is. It's the distance of two Ironman races combined into one event, which means a 4.8-mile swim, a 224-mile bike ride, and then running the distance of two marathons: 52.4 miles. It is also something that doesn't actually exist. My brother made it up to challenge himself and honor his friend. (I know, I know, we don't get him either.) In addition, not only was the distance for each event doubled, but Devin would be doing this completely unsupported on a loop through his city, only stopping at home occasionally to refuel, charge his phone, and change clothes between the swim, the bike, and the run portions.

When he talked about the event, my brother was really humble about it, sharing from the beginning that he wasn't sure he could even finish it. He wasn't sure his legs would hold out or that he wouldn't "bonk," a runner's term for complete exhaustion of mind, body, and soul. But he was absolutely going to try because Wyatt would have attempted something so bold and audacious, and it was the best way he knew to honor his friend. He didn't actually care about not finishing the event because for Devin, the failure was in not trying it at all. His mantra became, "Fear the thing; do the thing."

On the day of the event, a few of us joined in by doing our own version of athletic events, posting pics, and messaging Devin in a show of solidarity. When it came time to start the run portion, the double marathon, Devin was about twenty hours in, having completed the swim and the bike portions overnight and without sleep. He opened a web call that people could join while he ran, talking with one another and keeping him company. One of his Peace Corps teammates, who also felt a strong connection to Wyatt, was there the entire time my brother ran, a full Saturday, sometimes talking and sometimes just working in the background, but he kept that connection the whole time.

I logged in for a while out on my own eleven-mile walk to hear Wyatt's mom and best friend telling stories from his childhood. As a background soundtrack to every story shared, we could hear Devin's feet plodding along on the asphalt as he ran mile after mile. Every so often, the clomping of his feet would stop and we would ask if he was okay, if he was still there. "Yeah, I'm here. I'm okay," he would pant through labored breaths. He'd just switched to running on the grass, but he was still going, wearing Wyatt's high school track jersey that Wyatt's mom had sent to Japan just for that day.

With about three hours left in the run, Devin's energy started to wane, and he was getting noticeably fatigued. Devin's college triathlon coach and teammates were on the call sharing the perfect tips and encouragement from fellow athletes. They reminded him of the feat he was attempting and told him how astounded they were at how he was holding up. They gave him tips for pacing and foot placement and simply talked just to distract him. Wyatt's family and friends from South Dakota reminded him that Wyatt was with him and would be so proud of the race he was running.

As the miles became fewer, the energy on the call changed to pure anticipation. More people joined, some popping in and out to make dinner and put kids to bed, but the countdown was on to the finish. Our family and Devin's best friends from growing up joined, along with some of his college friends. We counted down the last bits of distance together, ten, nine, eight, seven . . . , cheering and crying as he completed event mile 281 in just under thirty-four hours. He had done it. He had completed the full distance of two Ironman triathlons.

When he set this goal and put it on social media for all to see, he had no idea if he would even finish this ridiculously huge thing he was attempting. Yet even knowing the high potential that he would fall short of the end goal, he invited others to join in on the journey with him. As it turns out, it may have been the presence of those witnesses to his potential failure who provided him the energy and the strength to keep going. Devin knew it was a huge undertaking, one that could have scared him away from attempting it at all. Which is what made it worth the doing for him. *Fear the thing; do the thing.*

Is there a place in the journey that you get held up or even stop because you feel like the only outcome is to fail? What is it that even if you fail to reach a set end result, would still mean you grow, learn new skills, and stretch yourself as a person? What is one step you can take to move in that direction of greater courage, and of doing the thing?

If my brother had gone into the experience thinking of the outcomes as binary, either succeed or fail, he may never have done it. Instead, his intention and his motivation were to honor his friend and to help others remember their loved one in the process. He was only ever going to succeed at that. Wyatt's mom was deeply moved by her son being honored in this way, and the rest of us were left inspired to slay our own dragons.

CHAPTER SIX

It Scares You

The summer I spent in Mexico was my first time away from home. The day before I left, I was up until two o'clock in the morning packing, but also fretting and crying. A few friends came to say goodbye, and I was teary eyed most of the night, talking through my anxiety and fears about missing the summer with them and heading into the strange unknown of the summer ahead. On the car ride down the next morning, I was in full crying hangover mode, sleeping sprawled across the back seat of our Suburban while my parents delivered their firstborn child away from home for the first time.

You already know it turned out okay—the best few months of my life. That's one of the most challenging parts about fernweh; the fear of taking the leap can sometimes frighten us away from ever actually doing it. How many times have you had a desire to lean into something, only to let your lack of skill and experience, the opinions of others, or the fear of failing keep you from taking the first step? Author Betty Binder says, "Everything I've ever done that was ultimately worthwhile . . . initially scared me to death." Peter Hollins puts it this way: "If you wait until you're ready, you'll be waiting the rest of your life."

Recently, I revealed the idea of following your fernweh to a friend, who is also a creative, and as we talked through what fernweh meant, he said that he felt like his fernweh is to write a book. He is a skilled visual artist, a practiced and confident musician, and a thoughtful and insightful verbal communicator. Art, he explained, is easy for him, almost second nature. It doesn't scare him the way writing a book does. A book feels big, challenging, and scary.

That's how I felt the year I turned forty. The year of the train horn outside my window, the loneliness, and the year I knew I needed to dream bigger. *A year on the road, to explore.* My fernweh was calling me.

It almost felt impossible to accomplish, even impossible to begin. *Could I really leave everything behind and just travel for a year?* I would have to talk to my manager at work about working remotely (well before remote work was the norm), put all my things into storage, go back to the house I grew up in, and then travel the world with no real home. For a year. At the end of the day, I would be relocating my life of fifteen years to a city I hadn't lived in for almost twenty. And I might not ever find my way back there.

Following my fernweh would mean I'd have to do all the things associated with a big move, from change of address to finding a new hair stylist to making local friends. I had a dog, JoJo, my best buddy, and worried how this would be for him.

While I would be out enjoying and traveling on one trip, I would need to be looking ahead, researching to schedule and plan the logistics for future trips. It would take time and money, neither of which was bottomless, both of which had to be budgeted. I would need to somehow keep working my full-time job, so all of the planning would be done on my own time in the after-work hours and weekends.

It was daunting and scary. And yet, I knew that life would be almost unbearable if that call had gone unanswered and I never took a leap of faith. The call of my fernweh would continue to haunt me all the days of my life if I ignored it.

That's not to say that anything that scares you is your fernweh, so hear me on that. We have been designed with an internal warning system to know when things are not right. Gut feeling, logic, intuition, or wise counsel. However you acquire the knowledge that something is unsafe for your life is yours to own and listen to. This is not the same thing as feeling nervous about failing, being judged, or lacking in skill and resources. Only you will recognize the difference between the healthy-warning-of-danger kind of fear and the feels-too-big-to-accomplish kind. Both can stop us from proceeding, and in many cases, one should halt us. However, one should be a hurdle we figure out how to get over, under, or around.

There's a balancing act to fernweh, too. Sometimes we have to set it aside for a bit to focus on our priorities, whether they be career, family, or health. And that's okay; just don't put your fernweh in a box in the back of your heart and forget about it. Leave it out where you can see it and schedule time to come back to it.

One of my favorite quotes of late is from a speech given by U.S. President Theodore Roosevelt at the Sorbonne in Paris in 1910, called "Citizenship in a Republic." This particular section is often quoted, and referred to as "The Man in the Arena." I've updated some of the pronouns to make it a bit more universal.

> It is not the critic who counts; not the [person] who points out how the strong [one] stumbles, or where the doer of deeds could have done them better. The credit belongs to the [one] who is actually in the arena, whose face is marred by dust and sweat and blood; who strives valiantly; who errs, who comes short again and again, because there is no effort without error and shortcoming; but who does actually strive to do the deeds; who knows great enthusiasms, the great devotions; who spends [one]self in a worthy cause; who at the best knows in the end the triumph of high achievement, and who at the worst, if [they] fail, at least fails while daring greatly, so that [their] place shall never be with those cold and timid souls who neither know victory nor defeat.

Neither you nor I are the kind who intend to live our lives as a cold or timid soul who knows neither victory nor defeat. That is not who we are.

By now, you hopefully have a sense about what big, audacious ideas and dreams are scaring you. You are having the feels-too-big-to-accomplish kind of fear about them. Your fernweh may be wrapped in there somewhere.

Spend some time in that place in your heart and mind. If you're ready, write the dream down, and next to it, write all the things that cause fear with that particular dream. If you are someone who prays, pray through them with God. Ask him to change your dream or to open impossible doors. See what he does. The fun of knowing God is seeing how creative he can be with us—paving paths to what's possible. He's the king of impossible beginnings.

A verse from the Bible that carried great hope and power for me as I pursued my fernweh was Habakkuk 1:5, "Look at the nations and watch—and be utterly amazed. For I am going to do something in your days that you would not believe, even if you were told."

Utterly amazed. Completely astounded and filled with wonder. Be encouraged in your dreams and in the seeming impossibility of them. Those kinds of dreams are God's specialty. Those kinds of dreams are the ones you were made for.

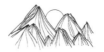

Summary: Discover Steps

- Define fernweh in your own words.
- Write down your personal fernweh.
- Give yourself permission to enjoy it just because you love it.
- Understand that failing can help you level up.
- Acknowledge and embrace that it might scare you.

PART 2

Plan Your Fernweh

CHAPTER SEVEN

Make Your Plan

You have probably heard the idea that the first step in solving a problem is to admit that you have one. Well, in no way am I inferring that fernweh is problematic; however, I think there is something powerful in acknowledging that something is what it is. By looking a belief, a desire, or a thought square in the eye and calling it by its name, we claim our space and our strength in that arena.

In May, the year I turned forty, I didn't yet have the word fernweh. But as soon as I recognized my latent desire for travel, the actions that needed to happen became so much clearer. The more I spoke to God about the dream of traveling for a year, the more I asked questions and gave myself permission to believe that something absurd might actually be possible, the closer it came to me.

I keep seeing myself being on the road next year. A year on the road, to explore. This wild pipe dream started as a theoretical speck on the horizon, and with each prayer, each time I didn't censor my own dream and allowed myself to see what was possible through God's eyes and abilities, the hope got bigger. And it got closer, more tangible, and more plausible.

As an act of faith that I might actually be able to pursue this fernweh dream of traveling for a year, I bought a calendar. Like, an actual paper calendar. My thought was to map out an initial plan, just a sketch for what the year could look like. It would stay flexible, but I knew I would have peace and clarity as to whether it was even a good idea if I started to envision what it might look like.

I started first by writing on the calendar in pen, putting events that would not be adjusted. These were mostly birthdays and holidays, same every year. Then, using pencil, with a large white eraser standing by, I wrote down events that were most likely solidified, things like work trips and personal vacations already in motion. I'd also found out the plans of others whose timelines would impact mine—for example, my mom asked that I house sit and dog sit while she was in Japan for a few weeks.

From there, I started to ask myself where I wanted to be and when. For example, both Seattle and San Diego were on the list, with big blocks of time open in February and in the summer. Based purely on weather, that was an easy choice. I could spend the month of February in San Diego and six weeks of summer in the Pacific Northwest, both Portland and Seattle. I also thought about events I wanted to be somewhere for, plotted those on the calendar, and built the schedule around that timing. My brother's birthday is in March, and by then my new nephew would have been about five months old, which was such a fun age to get time with him. So I planned a two-week vacation to Japan in late March.

There were other places that were on the initial list but didn't make the final cut. For example, I was most certain I had to get to Australia and work from our Sydney office, but that option had to step aside in favor of other ones. A big lesson I've learned along the way is that we can try something on for size and still decide to not buy it. Looking at an option from all sides and seriously considering it does not commit us to move forward with it. Saying no and walking away is an option, even after careful consideration. Understanding that principle has changed how I make decisions in my life. It leaves space for the, *Well, wait a minute. What if . . . ?*

Even though there were still so many things that needed to fall into place, I believed enough to test the theory by spending money on a calendar and mapping out what a potential plan could look like. When I did that, it didn't seem so big, so overwhelming, or so impossible. Putting pencil to paper, letting the dream become something I could design, made it so much more real. That calendar could easily have ended up just ideas in the recycle bin, but instead became the blueprint I went back to throughout the entire year. Always writing in pencil, staying flexible and adaptive to the plan morphing and changing as new opportunities and new challenges arose.

We spoke earlier about writing down what your fernweh could possibly be. You got bold and pushed past that inner critic and doubter to physically write down that dream, that drumbeat that you have going on inside of you. If you didn't give yourself space or permission to admit what that far-off calling is for you, can I encourage you again to do it now? If you did write it down, then are you ready to plan your own "calendar"? The nature of what is churning in you may not lend itself to a calendar plan. It may be an outline or a project planning tool. You may prefer colored pens and a notebook, or perhaps your go-to is a digital app.

First, what is that tool that makes something feel real for you? Go to that tool and write down what a few benchmarks on the journey would need to look like. You do not need to be an expert in all the steps right now. You have permission to be a novice, to be wrong, to be ignorant of what it will take. You have that permission from God himself, from people who have traveled that path before you, and from yourself. All you need to do is receive it.

For folks who find examples helpful, let's speak practically for a moment. If your fernweh is a dream for higher education, you may already know that you need to apply, be accepted, and start school. Granted, I went really simple here, and you may even already know more of the steps than that. Do you have a school in mind? Write it down. Do you have a date you want to start in mind? Write it down.

If you are a person of faith, I would also bring God into those conversations. Tell him your big, audacious, *it would take a miracle* desires. He knows you want that anyway. That's one of the best parts about God. He knows our deepest heart's desire, he loves us, and he wants us to discover for ourselves what it is and acknowledge that's what we want. He wants it to be a conversation.

See, here's the thing (I'm going to lean into my faith background a bit more here): God is the ultimate artist, architect, engineer, designer, and project manager. I mean, if you have ever read how the Tabernacle (a holy place for Jews in the Old Testament) was to be constructed in the book of Exodus, you know exactly why I say God has these traits. Talk about specifics. He provided exact measurements, materials, and colors in painstaking detail, yet it was all part of a gorgeous grand design that actually reflected his heart for his people. How do I know this? Auntie Beth. No Bible study content or workbook has ever impacted my faith as much as Beth Moore's book, *A Woman's Heart*. If you're into deep-dive studies, check it out. It will help you understand this element of God's character.

But instead of all this process, can't God just make something so? Can't he just "poof" it into being in a moment? Sure he can. Is there pleasure, meditation, and a connection to the created things because he takes the time to be a craftsman and not a magician? *Yes.*

See, being in on the planning is part of the fun for him, too. Let him into it. Let him help you make the decisions and the design by being your business partner, your editor, your mentor, and your co-conspirator. You don't have to go to him with a fully fleshed-out plan and get his approval to proceed or not. He's not a bureaucrat with a rubber stamp sitting behind a desk. He's a dreamer, too. And he's ready to help you plan your fernweh.

CHAPTER EIGHT

Learn to Trust

We talked early on that this conversation about following your fernweh would be approachable whether you share my faith or not. I hope you have found that to be true so far, no matter how our views may diverge at times. I have friends who believe that the universe will provide what they need or what they need will be manifested if they speak it aloud. I see and honor those views, and so appreciate the understanding that there is something greater than what we can physically see and touch.

To maintain your trust in our conversation, this is a heads-up that this next portion leans heavily into how we can trust God to provide everything we need. I also want to share how important it is to trust the journey and others who you invite into that journey. It just so happens that I invited God into mine.

On May 3rd, in my daily devotional, there were two seemingly opposing verses:

But I have this against you, that you have abandoned the love you had at first.

Revelation 2:4

You make known to me the path of life; in your presence there is fullness of joy; at your right hand are pleasures forevermore.

Psalm 16:11

After reading them, I wrote in my journal:

These seem the two sides of my heart right now. Abandoning you, and knowing there is peace right next to you. If I am to be out on the road for a year, I will need to be right next to you. Especially to see whose lives you will touch. I'm getting excited! But I need a few things to fall into place—a spot for JoJo, places to stay, approval from my manager. Can you make this a reality?

Forty on the road . . . What a cool adventure. Can you make it so?

Amen

A few years back, I had a friend who was really struggling to give themselves permission to lean into all God had for them. They were struggling to believe that their gifts and talents were truly as amazing as the rest of us knew they were. They struggled with crippling beliefs about identity and worthiness. All the potential God had for them was figuratively and almost literally laid out before them, and they wouldn't allow themselves to stretch out their hand and take it as the gift it was. Ultimately, they didn't trust God in the fulfillment of their fernweh calling.

I was agonizing over how to help them, feeling a desire within myself to take the promise of their incredible future on their behalf and just shove it into their hands. It was so clear to me and everyone who knew them. Just take it already. It's for *you*! But we cannot receive a gift on someone else's behalf. As I was struggling to find my place in helping this dear friend, God gave me a vision during a time of prayer and meditation that has become a benchmark in my faith and a promise from God to me. If this idea of a "vision" is new for you, I'll say it's like a dream, except you see it and experience it in your thought life while you are awake. Here is what I saw:

In my vision, this friend and I pull up in front of a huge mansion on a warm and sunny day with the sunroof of their car open, dance music playing, and we are laughing together. We've arrived at an estate with a circular driveway, the kind you pull in on one side, roll around in front of the house, and then leave on the other side. The home is light and Mediterranean, the landscaping mature and green, the driveway has light stone, and there could easily have been a giant fountain in the center circular part. It is Papa's house, God's house. We've come to see our Father. Filled with excitement, I hop out on the passenger side, bounding toward the entrance and closing the car door all in one motion. The music has stopped, and my friend is standing on the other side of the car, in the space between the driver's seat and the car door, elbow on the propped-open door, keys in hand.

I reach the front door. It's huge and heavy, the kind of door with just one enormous round handle in the middle of the panel. As my hand begins to push it open, I look back to see my friend getting back into the car. "I can't. I just can't," they say, breaking eye contact with me and restarting the car. I enter Papa's house with the sound of dance music overflowing from the open windows once again and the car pulling away behind me.

Toward the back of house, down some stairs, and overlooking the resort-like pool and tall trees in the backyard, I find Papa in his study. It's a grand yet homey room with high ceilings, tall arched windows, dark walls, and shelves filled with books and gathered treasures lining every wall. It's somehow light and antique feeling at the same time. I toss myself into an oversized saddle brown leather armchair, feet plunked onto the ottoman of the same color.

"Hi Papa," I begin. He's standing in the center of the room, looking over materials and plans laid out over a counter-height worktable in the middle of the room. It's like mission control, with a classic literature feel. The afternoon sun shines through the windows, lighting up the table, his hair, face, and hands. As he glances at what's in front of him, he holds a steady smile as I catch him up on all my adventures, ideas, thoughts, and learnings. He nods in understanding, patience, pride, and joy at my happiness and growth, at how much I've been enjoying the life he's created for me to get out and conquer. He is overjoyed at who I am becoming and how relaxed I am in his company and care.

When I have shared every last ounce of excitement and updates, he says to come and see what he is working on. By this time, we have sunk so comfortably into my storytelling that I now have to swing my legs off the arm of the chair I've been sitting in to leave my spot and join him at his worktable. He pulls out a bundle of long rolled-up papers, like an architect's house plans or a captain's map, and unrolls them on the table. He begins to lay out a design he is working on next, and how my journey, experience, and gifts intersect with his plans. He asks me to bring all of what I'm doing to partner with his next steps.

The vision ends there with the two of us hovered over his table, him sharing the next steps in his plan with me. What God has affirmed for me so many times when I recall this image is that not only is Papa the Creator and King over heaven and earth and all the designs within it, but I am his daughter. And as his daughter, I am an heir to all that he has and all that his kingdom contains. So for me to burst through the front door, into his office, and throw my feet up on the furniture—that is something we do in a house that we know is home, that is ours, that we feel a sense of ownership in. The Lord delights in us having that level of comfort and entitlement when it comes to being his daughters and his sons.

Being an heir to the Kingdom of heaven also means owning the responsibility to steward and to grow that Kingdom. See, Papa has big plans for all of us. Yes, we get to enjoy all the delights of being part of his lineage, and we also get to be—must be—a partner and a leader in how we care for his creation. Which means fully embracing all you have been given and going big. Sharing your dreams, joys, excitement, and failures with God and letting him delight in hearing them. And then hearing him when he gives you the strategic and valued part you have to play in his grand design. Recognizing the sense of honor and confidence that comes with knowing the high places you are called to, and how those high places ultimately lead to the service of God and others.

Here's the other thing about fernweh. I can't think of a single person's fernweh I know of that doesn't somehow build up and serve others. By its nature, I personally don't believe that for something to truly be the deep drumbeat of your heart, to be the thing that calls to you from the faraway places, it can be purely selfish. Every fernweh story I know either directly serves others or helps to free people to see the higher places they are called to themselves. By its nature, our fernweh calls us into the freedom of "out there" not only for ourselves, but for others we encounter along the way.

This is where you get to reflect on your understanding of your place in the grand design. Who are you when you roll up to your Father's house? Are you out in the driveway, feeling like an uninvited trespasser, hesitant to set foot onto this estate that is actually yours? Are your legs propped over the arm of the chair as you excitedly share your thoughts and plans with God? Are you at the worktable ready to hear what's next? Do you struggle to believe there is a big plan at all? Do you balk at the idea of God as a loving Creator?

The truth is, any of these are okay if that's exactly where you are in your journey and process. Be there; just don't be stuck there. If you speak to God at all, ask him to reveal the truth about you in that exact place, and the truth about who he is and where he is, there with you. If you don't believe in him, then ask yourself what you do believe about your part to play here on this earth, as you most certainly have a part to play.

If you need to do some of that work before you write down or map out your plan, that's okay. It might be a quick reflection or prayer in the moment, or it might be several conversations with a mentor or counselor. Be where you are and work through it. Just please, don't get back in the car and drive away from what you have been promised. This is your life, your house, your inheritance, and your Papa. He wants good things for you, and to be with you in the enjoyment of experiencing those good things. Invite him to be part of your discovery and part of your plan.

Oh, and whatever happened to the friend who was struggling to embrace the gifts and destiny God had for them? They ran for a while, avoiding, doubting, and distracting. But now they are working full-time doing exactly the thing they were created to do, growing in their skills and impact every day. And wondering why it took them so long to make the leap in the first place.

Why did I share this vision with you as part of the process to planning your fernweh? The way my story goes is that the more I trusted God to help me with the pieces falling into place, the more they did. I want to be mindful about not saying that as though it's a formula, as it most certainly is not. I have seen too many times where people of faith treat their personal lived experience as a formula that can be overlaid onto the lives of others in a similar situation. We can share experiences and ideas, but it is a fine line between sharing our stories and overstepping the boundary into formulaic solutions. When I share my experience of trusting God in the planning phase, it is my story, my history, and my truth. Yours will most certainly be a different story and one I would love to hear about and learn from.

Let's give each other and those around us the space to write their own story, to plan, make mistakes, and discover the hidden paths along the journey. Let's celebrate the wins, help to pick each other up from the stumbles and fight for our own and each other's belief in what's possible. The more we learn to unravel and undo our judgement of the steps and process of another, we will find that the loud voice of self-judgement will begin to quiet as well. Did you catch the nuance there? In case you didn't, part of why you are judging yourself and stopping your own forward momentum is because you are judging other people and their journey.

If you read that last bit and felt the sting of recognition, spend some more time there. Pray, seek wise counsel, read the words of Jesus or of Paul about how to see others' experiences. I would recommend starting with Romans 12:1–2.

For me, it really was true that the more I got excited, trusted God with the big pieces that needed to fall into place, and took unfamiliar steps, the more the picture came into focus. The truth is I was still struggling with feelings of uncertainty, loneliness, and abandonment. My fernweh journey wasn't all tied up in a perfect package. It was messy, *and* it was good.

In May of that year, I was still wrestling with a lot of doubt, not just about the potential journey, but about myself and who I was as a human. I questioned some of my relationships, the choices I had made in life until then, and sometimes even who I was. But by June, and especially July, so many pieces of the puzzle were coming together in big sections that I was beginning to see the whole picture.

I shared the idea with some close friends, and they were all in support of me. Someone whose support I really needed was my mom's. A major part of the plan rested on her willingness to welcome me back into her house so I could have a home base as I traversed the country and the globe for a year. It would be a major change for her, asking her to accommodate not just me, but my stuff and JoJo as well. She would have an additional, very gregarious, and often feisty, daughter living back at home, and an equally feisty "grandpuppy," as she affectionately called him.

We sat down to talk, and I shared with her the why of this adventure, the reasons behind it, what the pieces were that still needed to fall into place, but most importantly, her part in it. Not just the logistics, but her part in the bigger purpose. I was barely done sharing the initial explanation, fully expecting a landslide of detailed and logistical questions, when she jumped in. "Absolutely," she said. "I love this idea. I'm in, yes."

What's funny is that this may quite possibly be the biggest ask I've ever had of my mom, and it was also the fastest yes I've ever gotten from her. The question I'd been the most nervous to ask her, the most doubtful of a yes, was the most resounding yes she's ever offered. Doesn't that tell us something about when fear and doubt prevent us from even asking in the first place? That yes we need could just be one anxiety-filled conversation away. How many times have you not bothered to even pose the question because you assumed a denial was inevitable?

I had to keep riding this wave of surprising results into a conversation with my manager. See, I needed the green light from work as well, especially to move around the country regularly, while continuing my job and working out of the offices in the different cities I'd hoped to visit. This conversation had a high likelihood of being a showstopper, which made it all the more difficult to even begin. But somehow, I gathered the needed gumption and shared with her the vision and the reasons for an idea like this. It did provide the opportunity for greater management oversight and presence, which was a benefit to the organization as well. So I shared the idea, and paused. Her response? "I think this sounds incredible, and I will live vicariously through you." Approved.

From there, it was all logistics. For example, I had a house full of furniture. Did I keep it and store it? Sell it all? Give it away? It turns out I did a combination of all of the above. I had to think through what would cost more to store for a year than to replace in a year, and vice versa. These types of practical considerations all came up, even in the dreaminess of following my fernweh. I had to find a great doggie daycare and boarding option for JoJo, there would be paperwork to submit, and he would need a new vet.

But as these questions all began to be worked out, the excitement of what was actually about to happen started to build. It hit me that this crazy, insane, impossible idea from less than a year before was now actually a reality that I was planning for and telling people about. The more I shared that I was leaving the place I'd been for fifteen years, the more excited I became. At the end of August, the night before I left San Jose, I wrote this prayer in my journal:

Off we go, God! I trust you. Amen.

Off we go. I trust you. In these months of preparation and planning, the God of heaven and earth earned my trust so profoundly that I rearranged my life within the framework of that trust. I've heard it said that men fall in love all at once—one big decision and they just know. In contrast, it's been said that women fall in love through a process of many small decisions, trust being built up over time, before they commit their life to that person.

The period of planning, of God filling in the gaps, solving problems, and answering my questions was overwhelmingly profound for my trust and love of him. This era of making the decision to travel for a year and getting ready for a massive life change created a new dynamic in our relationship that can never be undone. It was an overwhelming adventure that was only possible both internally and externally because of God's presence throughout the entire experience.

In my life now, I sometimes crave opportunities to trust him in bigger ways. Since the one big year of travel, there have been plenty of those chances to put all my trust in God because another big adventure was rolling in. Another loud drumbeat was calling from the distance beyond. But first, let's talk about this fortieth year on the road, because then you'll understand how I came to the place where the only option was to choose more adventure—to continue to follow my fernweh.

CHAPTER NINE

Get the Right Tools

As you may have gathered by now, my favorite part of this process is the ideas, celebration, and even frivolity of following your fernweh. I mean, could anything be more fun than dreaming about a mountain to climb and the joy of making your way to the top of it, arms pumped in the air in victory? But this is also where we need some plain talk. To get to the mountaintop, the podium, the leveling up, you have to be willing to dig into the mundane and the practical. And the reality of any journey is that there are required tools for every path.

In Moana's case, she packed food, her oar, and of course, her sailboat. As a voyager with more contemporary options, I needed luggage, my passport, and other travel amenities. Equipping your- self with the right tools for your unique journey involves both indulgence and self-restraint. Have you ever known someone who takes up a new hobby and invests a lot of money up front on related equipment that might be above their skill or commitment level? Sometimes their progression in that passion rises to the level of equipment they have, and other times that stuff ends up in a garage, spare room, or local marketplace site. I have absolutely done that personally.

In college, I switched from skiing to snowboarding, which I tried a couple times and then *had* to have my own board. I started that next winter season with a brand-new snowboard, which I then used a total of six days on the mountain over the next two years, only to later tuck into a closet, then the garage, and eventually pass it on. I overstepped my skill set and interest level.

What's worked for me since then is to start small and simple. To see how I really operate in that space and then decide what the next tool is to invest in. With travel as my passion, there are many ways to make the journey easier, but my investment in ways to save time and stress has evolved over time.

I first began to sort out what was worth paying extra for and what wasn't by flying Southwest Airlines along the West Coast. For me, paying the extra amount for their early bird check-in was always worth it. When I fly airlines that have an economy-plus option, that's never worth it for me. I don't need the extra leg room; however, I like the option to easily get up and move around, so I will pay extra for an aisle seat. The amount I'm willing to pay to have my time and comfort intact has increased a bit over time. Nothing extravagant, just recognizing what makes the journey more efficient.

The other place this has come into play for me is with luggage. I'd been rattling around with a soft-sided mid-range suitcase for a long time. When I eventually stepped into a world with coworkers coming and going from all over the world on a weekly basis, I discovered the value of investing in the best luggage for how I move and pack. It was pricey and well worth it.

My new work life had included several seven-to-ten-day trips to Europe, all with a carry-on, so it was time to upgrade to better equipment. To be honest, I wrestled with feelings of guilt and frivolity when I first considered the new price point of nice luggage, but then it occurred to me that if I were a competitive runner, I would invest in the best footwear. If I were a professional photographer, I would upgrade my cameras as the technology improved. Same situation here, as I had become a seasoned and sometimes professional traveler. It was time to upgrade my tools and technology. I've never since had difficulties with dragging bags across an airport or really had to give my luggage a second thought. That's when you know you've invested in something that takes things up a level, when it makes life so easy you don't have to think about it anymore.

As you get into the community of your particular fernweh, learn from others about the best insiders' tips, tools, and tricks. For travel, that means the loyalty clubs, the best websites for booking, the best times to book and how to avoid what the masses do. Find out what that is for you. Meet people in your community, research online, experiment, talk to customer service, and ask good questions. I joined a few key loyalty clubs that resulted in free hotel stays and flights. No need to overwhelm yourself with every option, but find out what you need to know.

Then be sure to be a good member of the community by sharing resources you find in return. A great place to keep this dialogue going is online. Through places like Reddit, Twitter, and Instagram, people with common interests have found not only resources, but community. I recommend being an active participant in the conversation. Yes, that means liking the content you see, but it also means engaging with it through comments, sending a private message to the content creator, or tagging another member of the community in something you like. For me, this has helped to more accurately adjust the type of information I see (oh, those algorithms) as well as create better conversations with folks I learn from. And I'm in there doing my best to add value, too.

Now, when it comes to organizing the tools you need for your fernweh, admittedly, I am a procrastinator by nature. I think it's a mix of both anxiety and being more intrigued by other seemingly more interesting things. If I think too much about all the tasks and projects that need to be done, I get overwhelmed, stressed, and then the process is no longer fun, which takes the whole purpose away for me. It has to be fun.

My first international stop on my year of travel was London. I would be working from our London office for a month, while also taking shorter trips to six countries and several different climates. I had sold or stored all my things, worked out all the details for JoJo, and was staying at my mom's house in the room she was renting to me by the week when this trip kicked off.

It was the night before I was scheduled to leave, and my mom was going to drop me at the airport shuttle stop at 5:30 the next morning. I'd made my packing list and had visualized in my mind how it would all fit in the medium-sized suitcase, but when my mom came by my door that night to check on my progress, there was nothing packed or even laid out.

Before I tell you the level of stress this caused her, let me share that for context, my mom packs for an international trip about a week in advance. So this situation was completely out of her realm of understanding. She started with casual questions about how I was coming along in the packing and then passed by again later to ask what jacket I was planning to take with me. The answers to those were, "good" and "not sure yet." When she came by again around 8:30 p.m. to see when I was planning to start packing and I told her I was packed in my mind and would do it in a bit, she threw her hands up in the air and said she was going to bed. I did, in fact, cut that packing situation a bit too close and was rushed in the morning, leaving about twenty minutes later than planned for the shuttle.

I've learned a few things since that less-than-stellar packing performance. Most importantly, how to become a project manager for myself. Understanding how long things take, how far in advance they need to be done, and in what sequence they need to get done will change your life. If you already have your systems on lock for this, first, I'm in awe of you. And second, if you have ideas beyond what you see here, please share. This is by no means an exhaustive list as much as it is personal learnings.

To keep organized, I used to have a calendar, a to-do list, and a shopping list. This became too many places to keep track of things, especially as my travel started to include two short trips in a week's time. I felt all over the place. What worked for me was finding a tablet of preprinted weekly calendar templates. Yes, paper. For those who have switched to digital, this idea may make your skin crawl. It's one of the few places I'm still analog. That, and I'm all about a physical Bible and journal. We like what we like.

This little piece of paper helps me organize each week in advance, getting a visual on all the commitments on my time, and then allowing room to slot in things that need to get done. For example, if there is a due date for something and I am busy in the days leading up to it, then I intentionally block out its own time and space for when the work itself will be accomplished. It's also where I collect shopping lists and random ideas.

We all have our methods, but if you're going to follow your fernweh, you will actually have to make time for the "following it" part. This may mean a mix of building it into your schedule and reprioritizing other efforts you currently give your time to, even for a season. It also means gathering the right tools to help you implement your journey. If one of the tools you need is, in fact, time, then make that a priority.

And if what you carve out time for is to just daydream, research, journal, and process, that is part of the journey, especially in the beginning and in times of transition. Give yourself permission to do that part of it. You may not come home from a coffee or a walk armed with a five-part business plan, but your heart will be fuller, and you'll have taken a step to get where you are going. You are worth it. That drumbeat you feel in your chest is worth following. And it will only get louder.

CHAPTER TEN

Let People Into Your Dream

In the days before I left San Jose for the year of travel, I had several gatherings with friends to make sure I could see everyone before leaving. As it was right before the big fortieth birthday, it was the perfect excuse to celebrate both my birthday and the start of the adventure year. My cousin likes to tell me that I'm the most frivolous person she knows, and I own that sense of lighthearted fun completely. Author and speaker Bob Goff describes his adventures as "capers," which has not only become a descriptor of the kind of fun I like to have, but a personal goal to create capers and invite other people to join in on the fun.

Two of my dearest friends in the world, Ben and Jessica, are the king and queen of having capers with me. They are the kind of friends who help you believe anything is possible, and when you are with them, it feels like you are one of the best people they have ever known. I one hundred percent feel the exact same way about them. They were preparing to leave the city at the same time as me, heading for a work assignment overseas in Europe, and yet, in the midst of their own preparations, they ensured my departure was as magical as possible.

We had a picnic in the park. "Forty and farewell," I called it. An artist friend helped with the fun by designing a fortieth birthday logo: a laurel wreath around the number forty. In true frivolous fashion, I had it printed onto blue plastic tumblers for the park picnic, and onto wine glasses and T-shirts for the birthday wine tasting weekend in my hometown that was yet to come. Because, who doesn't need their own birthday logo? Ben and Jess helped to set up and tear down the party. They were there for all the fun and all the prep for the fun. They are a big part of this fernweh story and, funny enough, now living in the country where fernweh originates from. They were also among the first on the scene in my hometown where a small group of friends gathered for a full weekend itinerary to celebrate turning forty and the launch into the yearlong travel adventure.

Ben and Jessica did all this because of the significance and longevity of our friendship, yes. I've known them for about twenty years, and we have encouraged and built each other up along the way for all of life's changes and adventures. But they are also into capers, and supporting other people as they succeed. They are the kind of friends who want to be part of an adventure, even if it's not their own, and even if it means cheering from the sidelines while other people have their moment.

Don't you think a lot of us are like this? It's the reason we clap and cheer when a couple is announced at their wedding, and why we clink glasses for them to kiss. It's why we go out of our way to create elaborately themed and decorated parties, or go through all the steps to throw a surprise party. We want to be part of someone's joy. It is an honor when they invite us to be in on the fun of their happiest moments. When we love someone, when we believe in them, we want to celebrate them. And when we are the ones celebrating, it is made so much sweeter when our people are with us, in person or in spirit.

In a small stroke of genius amidst planning for these birthday and pre-departure celebrations, God gave me the idea to capture the words of people I encountered along the way. I bought a journal, wrote an introduction note in the first few pages, and took it with me on every trip. As I met up with old friends on the journey and got to meet new friends along the way, everyone was invited to write in the book. It was a way for them to mark the moment they helped send me on the journey or met me out on the trail.

Some wrote a sentence or two, some wrote pages, some drew, and some pasted art, pictures, or notes. There were entries in it from California to New York to London. When meeting up with friends along the way, I would have the book with me in my bag, pulling it out, and sometimes waiting quietly across a restaurant table for someone to add their thoughts. It was not only a way to remember and document the journey, but a way to be comforted and encouraged when I felt especially alone. Having it then, and still to this day, was worth any level of extra effort or any discomfort in asking someone new to write in it. It was worth it.

In one of those subtle details that God often provides just for the fun of it, I found a journal where the cover design included the Thoreau quote, "Live the life you've imagined." I wrote in the first few pages:

Now to him who is able to do immeasurably more than all we ask or imagine, according to his power that is at work within us.

Ephesians 3:20

Dear family and friends,

This note is to people who have known me my whole life, shared part of my life in different places, and to those I have yet to meet on this journey.

The God of heaven and earth put a dream in my heart to go. To see this world he made and the people he put in it. You are one of those people.

This year of adventure will be filled with stories, fun, hardships, and life lessons—and I can't wait for all of it! Can't wait to share it with you, to have you be part of it!

This book is the first step. I need your hearts and stories and fun and encouragement to take with me. To remind my heart of home and to capture new places that will become like home.

Will you write a note, a Bible verse, a quote, a memory, or even draw a picture? I will look at these often. And it will help me to think of you and pray for you!

Come and meet me on the road!

Love, Kindle

I thank my God every time I remember you.

~Philippians 1:3

#followingmyfernweh
#ayearontheroad

In the Old Testament, when something significant happened for the Jews of Israel, they would build an altar, or a stone shape, to remember where they had been and what happened there. This book felt a bit like a roving altar, a way to remember and mark the journey along the way. I would absolutely encourage this step for anyone in the process of following their fernweh. Even as you get started, be intentional about marking the important moments. It might be a note in a journal, a mental image, or a photo that you put in a fernweh album on your phone. When someone gives you encouraging words about where you are going, capture them somewhere. You will use them, like rest stations on an endurance course. Gather them early and often. I can promise you will need them.

I sure did, at different times and for varying reasons. These words in my little book:

Told me to be brave.

You have a love of life and are fearless to try and experience new things. It's like you stare down where you are and you choose hope and love. –Nick

Journey on, pilgrim. Walk boldly. –Missy

Just keep saying YES!! –Atina

Made me laugh.

When you are sad, turn your frown upside down. –M, age six

Have a awesome trip to where ever your giong (sic) to. I'm going to give you my best drawing ever. (Arrow pointing to a drawing taped into the book) –K, age ten

Reminded me I was loved.

You're always loved here.
Come home anytime and often.
We'll be waiting with open arms. –AM

We've got to remind ourselves to let people in for each new part of the journey. It might be different people who join us on different parts of the path. As I was working on the second edit of this book, a dear friend, Allegra, asked somewhat hesitantly if I was planning to have some folks read it before it went to be published. She was quite sheepish in how she posed the question, and since she and I have a super honest and supportive communication style, I just asked her, "What's happening with you here?" with a swirl of my hand in her direction. "Are you suggesting that I really should do it, or are you asking if you can be a reader of an early version?"

"Mmmm . . . yeeahhh. I really wanna read it," she said in a squeaky voice. As my dear friend, and as a writer and creative herself, she actually wanted to have a sneak peek of what I was working on. She wanted to be in the inner circle. She was so excited for me. She just didn't want to insert herself or ask to be part of it unless she was invited and welcome. I sent her a couple of sections right away, and her feedback was empowering.

Do you have people to let into your dream as you start to pull the pieces together? Are there folks in your life who will help you do some of the heavy lifting, either emotionally or physically, to help push the boat away from the dock and get going? Invite them in. Let them share in the joy of the process. Planning your fernweh shouldn't take place in isolation. Now that you know what your fernweh is, allow others to be part of the dreaming and planning process. Besides, you'll want them there with you as you begin the adventure.

Summary: Plan Steps

- Every good journey takes some intentional planning.
- Following your fernweh requires trust.
- Invest in the tools that will make the journey smoother.
- Let people into your dream. They want to come along for the journey.

PART 3

Enjoy Your Fernweh

CHAPTER ELEVEN

There Will be Magic

Fernweh is a dream, a hope for something extraordinary, even magical, that we haven't yet discovered or experienced. We've talked about how to recognize and bring into focus what your fernweh is, along with some practical and strategic steps to actually get going and make it happen.

What I want to talk about next is how much joy, fun, and absolute delight there is in actually following your fernweh. Sometimes we can focus so much on overcoming the obstacles to get there that we miss the wonder. If it's really your fernweh, there will be fun and delight. There will be magic.

I had those magic moments and experiences around every corner being a nomad for a year. So you may be wondering, what did I actually do during this year of travel? Let me start by telling you that it was both one of the most incredible and challenging years I have ever had. Having the calendar to loosely plan the year was really helpful. Part of my goal for the year was to have a grand and unbelievable adventure. Another goal was to see where I would want to live after leaving Silicon Valley: what city could become my new home? So I planned a year of destinations and timing that allowed me to accomplish a mix of those goals. Wherever it worked, I linked something fun to a work trip, and I made sure to take time, even just a few hours, to enjoy wherever I was.

To start, I rented a spare room at my mom's house, and the first few days back there were over my fortieth birthday weekend, which also fell over the three-day Labor Day weekend. Friends came into town to celebrate with wine tasting in a party bus, a beach day, backyard BBQ, yummy dinners, and the frivolous T-shirts and wine glasses I'd had made for the occasion. It was epic and the perfect beginning to a year of adventure. As if the personal celebrations and puzzle pieces all falling into place were not enough of a gift, there were incredible blessings in my professional life at that time as well. Not only had my manager been fully supportive of this alternative living situation, there was one more unexpected piece yet to come.

I had been working in a field office for the organization in my role as a director, overseeing offices dotted throughout the western United States. The corporate headquarters were located in my hometown, where I was moving back to, and also where I was trained for my first role with this company. It was a full-circle experience, as I returned to my hometown that August and sat down in an office where I'd originally been trained almost two decades earlier. In the first meeting of that first morning back in that original office, my manager told me that districts were being rearranged and I would now also have the large bi-coastal offices. That meant Los Angeles, the San Francisco Bay Area, and New York. Turns out, it also worked to their strategic advantage that I could travel and spend time on the ground at the sites as well. And it meant even more frequent travel opportunities.

With this news, the travel year started with a long trip to the East Coast just a few weeks after my fortieth birthday weekend. While New York is still part of the same country as California, it is most definitely an entirely different world culturally. Every moment in Manhattan feels electric to me, every single time I'm there. The unrelenting street noise of taxis, jackhammers, people talking into headphones, and car horns. The visual input of neon signs, businesspeople in suits shaking hands and parting ways on the street, a new shop front and window display every few feet, and plastered-on posters for Broadway shows and concerts. The oddly delicious smell of subway brake dust as you pass over sidewalk grates.

Admittedly, it's super weird, but the smell of a train's tracks is one my favorite smells in the world. It's full of movement and potential and the convergence of people and all their worlds at the same time. It's cosmopolitan heaven.

I found myself energized and out of my element in New York just a few weeks after this yearlong adventure began. Like my instructor that summer all those years ago in Mexico, I had to observe how New Yorkers moved through the world in order to thrive in theirs. I wanted to blend in like a local, be mistaken for a

New Yorker. So I observed how they took up space on a sidewalk, queued at the coffee stand at Grand Central, waited for a ride app arrival, swiped their Metro cards through a station gate, and traveled on a commuter train with an oversized suitcase.

This is all socialized and known behavior for them as locals and can even vary depending on the borough you're in. Patterns in Brooklyn are different than Staten Island and different still from the Bronx. Which means even within the boundaries of New York City itself, there are vast cultural differences to be observed, learned, and adopted. For me, those were exactly the external experiences that led to the internal adventure I'd been seeking. To be pushed out of my comfort zone, to be on my toes, to learn to adapt in a new culture and a new space. It was pure magic, and I was just three weeks in.

The next stop on the plan for the year was actually back home. My mom had agreed to rent me her guest room by the week for that year so that I had a home base as I came and went. The entire year would not have been possible without that from her. She is an amazingly generous mama. In October, my nephew was due to be born, and my mom, Grammie, flew to Japan to be there to help with his three-year-old sister and to meet the newest member of the family. The timing was divine, and my mom was able to be in the room, across an ocean, to see her grandson take his first breath in this world. I stayed with her pup back home and relished all the stories and pictures that came from afar. My own travel was "grounded" for three weeks, almost a full month; however, being part of someone else's adventure didn't feel like a pause in my journey but an enrichment to it. An incredible reminder that as we pursue our own dreams it gives us the energy to share with others, too. That's part of the magic.

Something we haven't talked much about is that during all this time, I was still a single gal about town, hoping to find that great love. The all-immersive pursuit of my fernweh meant that I really wasn't worried about finding someone in the immediate future or even focused on it much at all. My life was already full of dreams, plans, and lots of novelty. I was falling in love with my own life. And so, of course, entered James.

In a thoughtful and unassuming message on a dating site, he introduced himself and piqued my interest. Initially just flirtatious and lighthearted, I didn't think much about it at first. By the time we connected through text, we were both traveling for work, sharing pics and airline stories, connecting naturally. Much like a lot of life in that part of the year, it felt breezy and whimsical.

He was someone who quickly felt like home, a kindred spirit from the start. We progressed at such a natural pace: texting, calls, and phone dates from our different cities. When our schedules lined up, we were able to sneak in an actual in-person date the week before I was about to leave for London. That date was, even to this day, the best first date of my life. Both of us felt like we were already invested and completely comfortable with where we were in the process. Not insecure or rushed, but exactly where we should be in the world, as much of that year of fernweh felt.

While I think we both felt the sting of just meeting each other and me then leaving for the other side of the world, James quickly became one of my biggest fans and supporters. Instead of feeling threatened by the distance, he created ways for us to continue to date and get to know each other from afar. He never once asked me to give up an adventure or an activity for his comfort or happiness while I was away. Instead, he poured into mine and embraced the journey with me. Which made it so much easier to want to include him and to make time for us along the way. I wrote about him in my journal in October, just before leaving for London:

Thank you for James. I am super into him. When I think he is going to fail me, he says or does the perfect thing. He is confident, and humble. I really like him.

So, with the giddiness of new infatuation in my heart, I boarded an overnight flight to London Heathrow Airport. This was the first trip I'd ever done like this, touching down in a new country with no friends or guide to meet me at the airport. It was completely up to me to get myself from the airport into the city, to Notting Hill, where I'd rented a room for the month.

Knowing London better now, the easiest thing would have been to take the Underground right into the city, which is also the most cost effective. But I had luggage and was nervous, so I decided to get a taxi to take me right to the flat. Only thing is, I needed cash, so I dragged a huge suitcase around the airport, found an ATM, paid exorbitant fees, found the taxi stand, and took one of London's famous black cabs into town.

Like New York, London's cab culture is its own world. The black cab drivers in London spend years studying the streets of the city—first by scooter, then by car—and can take you anywhere by memory. The idea of rideshare apps is truly insulting to them, flying in the face of their lengthy training and deep knowledge of London. They know everything about that city, and I tried to use the black cabs as much as possible, as it's truly part of the experience of being a Londoner.

After a four-hour shuttle ride, an overnight flight, U.K. immigration, luggage carousels, finding the taxis, a forty-five-minute ride into town, and roughly $100 later, I was at the curb in front of my flat. Now, you would think the first day in a new city would be pure magic. I mean, who hasn't seen the movie montage with an American gal twirling in a skirt and hat in the busy square of a foreign city, finally having made it to her dream destination?

However, that first overcast day I felt a little lost. I didn't know anyone in town to meet up with, my friends and family back home weren't awake yet, and I needed to unpack and get ready for work the next day, as I'd arranged to work remotely from the London office. So my day was spent buying groceries, figuring out the route to work, learning the bus system, and unpacking. Normal life stuff, just less familiar and a bit harder. I could not figure out the double-lock, skeleton-key front door situation at the flat. It's seriously a miracle that in the month I was there I managed to always make it into the apartment without help. Funny how the simplest things can be the most complicated and fear inducing. But I made it through that first day of getting settled and then through my first regular day of work. Somehow, I was reminded to thank God in my journal prayers that night:

November 2nd

Always giving thanks to God the father for everything, in the name of our Lord Jesus Christ.

Ephesians 5:20

Thank you, God, for this adventure.

Even when we are chasing our dream, going after our biggest adventure, and experiencing the magic, we can still be distracted, terrified, scared, and anxious. We still are who we are, so those old feelings of doubt that we wrestle with can still follow us. The presence of our greatest fear often means we're pointed in the right direction. If we aren't doing something that scares us and makes our hands shake, we're not going big enough. If we aren't doing something that makes our heart flutter because we're so nervous and so out of our comfort zone, then we may not be living as loud as we can be living right now.

The goal of my time in London was to really experience the city as a local, as well as use it as a home base for other travel throughout Europe. I was there for the month of November, and at the end of the first week, took the train by myself to Scotland for a weekend in Edinburgh. I left London from King's Cross Station, getting a picture at platform 9 ¾ before boarding the train for a lovely ride to a whole new country. On the train, I read my daily devotional, which offered these verses (bold portions are mine):

The one who sent me is with me; *he has not left me alone, for I always do what pleases him.*

John 8:29

*And without faith it is impossible to please God, because anyone who comes to him must believe that he exists and that **he rewards those who earnestly seek him.***

Hebrews 11:5–6

After reading these phrases and feeling they so perfectly fit with my experience in that moment, I wrote prayers in my journal:

November 6th

Hard to believe, but it's already the end of my first week in Europe! The days just fly by, and yet every moment is captured.

This experience is so incredible. I have to wonder often how I got here and why you were blessing me so much. My life and experiences are not always incredible. Not always this grand. But this is off the charts. Thank you, God. That's all I can say. Thank you.

Do you ever do that in the middle of something grand, pause and take a moment for gratitude and reflection? I find myself doing it more and more; perhaps it's age and experience? Perhaps it's having gone through enough times when things haven't worked out that makes gratitude and delight so much easier when a blessing comes our way. If you haven't tried this practice of mid-experience gratitude (not a very catchy phrase, but I'm going with it), look for an opportunity the next time you find yourself in the midst of something you feel blessed by. It's something I learned to do on this travel year and has become one of my more tangible spiritual practices.

The train arrived at Waverly Station in the center of Edinburgh in the early afternoon, warm light streaming into the station hall from skylights above. It was Remembrance time in the United Kingdom, which means images of red poppies were visible everywhere, on posters, lapels, and adverts. As I looked for the exit, an announcement came over the loudspeaker asking everyone to pause and observe one minute of silence to honor those who served and died in the wars. All of the activity in the station came to an unassuming and gentle pause. No footsteps, no transactions in shops, and no voices. The only movements were the empty escalators, waiting to transport travelers. After a minute, the announcer thanked everyone for their attention and the world resumed once again.

I came out of the station into the afternoon sun and took a walk from the city hub to my hotel, checking into a room for a weekend getaway by myself. This trip to Scotland was the first time I could remember ever vacationing like this, alone in a foreign country where I had no home base of people to connect with. It was especially significant because I had left my home base in a foreign country to go stay in a new foreign country, so it felt far away from something that was already far away. In London, I at least had a flatmate and coworkers around town. In Scotland, I had no one.

I was fine spending time by myself but also was lonely for people to talk to. I wasn't yet at a place where going to restaurants and bars alone was a familiar and comfortable activity. I started my weekend with a low-risk activity, taking one of the double-decker city tour buses around Edinburgh and having lunch at Greyfriars Bobby's Bar. I toured Edinburgh Castle and walked from that ancient stone fortress on a hill down the Royal Mile to Holyrood Palace. In the evening, I found a local pub on the corner of the street where my hotel was and went in to have a cider at the bar. Pretty soon, I found myself making friends with two couples and talking to them for hours. When the post-drinks hunger started to set in, we ventured together down the road to a fry place, and we had samples of fried everything late into the night. They were also all up visiting from London on a weekend getaway. The two women and I became fast friends, connecting on social media, and to this day, we are still connected. I have followed their lives getting married, moving, changing jobs, and it's one of those connections where it takes you a minute to realize how you even know each other in the first place. But we were bonded over this idea of culture, travel, and a fun night out on the town. They helped take Edinburgh from just a new place to explore to a city that I now love and can't wait to visit again.

During my second week in London, I'd convinced my friend, Charlotte, to fly from Chicago and meet me in Italy for a long weekend. We touched down at Fiumicino Airport within an hour of one another and hit the ground running, packing Rome and a trip to the Amalfi Coast into five days. We stayed first in a centuries-old apartment in the heart of Rome, in a neighborhood called Campo de' Fiori. The huge metal outer door to our apartment building opened right onto the narrow street, pulling us into the fun of the city as soon as we crossed the threshold.

Wandering through the cobblestone streets, passing by stands of fresh produce and flowers, with the smell of chestnuts being roasted by street vendors, I was astounded at how Rome somehow felt like make-believe. It was so much like being plunked down in the middle of a movie set that it simply had to be pretend. But it wasn't; it was now part of my real life, and strolling down those narrow cobblestone streets, I was reminded that had I never dreamed, or followed the call of that dream, I wouldn't be there in that very moment.

Our first stop in Rome was to Piazza Navona for a wine-filled lunch on a restaurant patio bordering a plaza, all centered around a fountain that may have been older than the country I was born in. My Italian coworker in London was from Rome and was emphatic that we have fried artichokes in Piazza Navona. That there was nothing in the world so delightful as a fried artichoke from Piazza Navona. (Imagine a lot of hand waving happening with this recommendation.) It was the right thing to follow her advice; I still dream about those artichokes to this day. From there, we soaked up all the culinary delights of Rome.

It was also truffle season, so we had truffle sauce or truffle oil anytime it was an option. We had gelato by Fontana di Trevi, tossing our coins into the newly renovated fountain, of course, guaranteeing we will return to the Eternal City one day. We drank red wine at every meal, which led to the very important personal discovery that I don't actually like Italian wine. We all have our things, *amiright*? One of the days, we had wine and lunched on pasta carbonara at a curbside café with a view of the Vatican.

Speaking of Vatican City, we spent the better portion of a day touring this surreal country. We got onto a last-minute walking tour, winding first through the streets around the Vatican and hearing about the politics and ruling family of ancient Rome. Then, wandering through the gardens inside the Vatican walls, we listened while our guide spilled the tea about the social dynamics and the art production process during the period when Michelangelo painted the Sistine Chapel. We walked the long hallway of the Map Room, astounded to learn of the Papal power plays that occurred when foreign dignitaries came calling. Finishing the Vatican tour in the Sistine Chapel was truly the icing on the cake after all we'd taken in. And then we entered Saint Peter's Basilica, where my mouth literally dropped open upon seeing the enormity and grandeur of the place.

Charlotte and I spent much of our time in Rome just walking around the city. The architecture, the small plazas, the hidden shops, the Tiber River running through the city center, the designer brands housed in ancient buildings, it's all a buffet for your senses. We walked around the outside of the Colosseum at dusk, with the late afternoon golden light coming over the top wall's edge and casting shadows on the east side of the building. Looking up to that top rim of the wall, I was reminded of my ancestors of faith who were sacrificed for sport in that place—sometimes used to light the night sky as human torches—and was moved to tears at how hallowed that ground was.

From Rome, we headed to the Amalfi Coast, taking the high-speed Frecciarossa train south to Naples, and from there catching a local train to a station near the town we were staying in. The local train was packed with folks who didn't speak English, and we didn't really know where we were going, so that ride was one of the more uncertain ones of my travels.

It was the off-season for the Italian coast, and the closer to the tourist cities the train got, the emptier the car we were riding in became. Eventually it was just me and Charlotte and an American couple who we came to find out were honeymooning in Italy. They also didn't really know where they were going, but we all got out at the same tiny train station, thinking we could catch a bus to Positano. No buses. In a mix of spotty English and Italian, we discovered that the man working the desk at the station had a brother-in-law who had a taxi, so a loud call in Italian and twenty minutes later, the four of us were sharing a ride into town.

Positano is built on a hillside with winding, often one-way, roads down to the water. Our hotel was on a hillside overlooking the southwest Italian coast, where we could sit on the balcony and smell the salt air of the Mediterranean. We ate lobster, we walked the windy roads on the sides of the cliffs, we shopped in tiny boutiques, chatting with shop owners who had sold to tourists for generations, and by Sunday night, Charlotte was en route home to Chicago, and I was back in my London flat getting ready for work the next morning.

This trip to Italy felt like I was living in the middle of a movie, less like my real life and more like floating. The sights, smells, tastes, textures, and colors all felt like the saturation had been dialed way up. Everything was vibrant, buzzing, and alive. It was the perfect culmination and demonstration of why believing in, planning for, and following my fernweh was worth it. I was exactly where I had dreamed of being, and where I was meant to be.

Have you felt like this before with things in your life that make you come alive, that feel like magic? When you follow your fernweh, everything has a vibrancy to it that most other aspects of life don't hold. While it isn't all magical all the time, you feel a sense of purpose and true enjoyment. That's where your fernweh lives. In the middle of that feeling. Watch for those moments and seasons of life—and embrace them. You might just find yourself falling in love with your own life.

CHAPTER TWELVE

Delight in the Adventure

If I learned anything from my year of travel, it is that sometimes the whole point is just to have fun. This journey is there for you to enjoy and to savor, to be fully present in the big and small moments, and in how you are growing and changing in the process. I also learned that our fernweh adventure can be made sweeter with frivolous details to add flourish and delight. For me, these moments came in the form of excursions and capers with friends along the way.

That third week in London, I soaked up all the city had to offer, and then took the fourth week off to spend Thanksgiving with Ben and Jessica, who had now moved to Germany and were settling into their new home there. Jess and I also made plans to take a two-night girls' trip to Paris, as neither of us had been to France.

We'd started making plans while I was in Italy with Charlotte; however, I woke up on Sunday morning of the Italy trip to the news of bombings in Paris. As friends woke up all over the world, messages of concern started coming in to make sure we were okay. We were hundreds of miles and another country away from Paris; however, it was scary to be far from home and feel somewhat exposed to terrorism in a foreign city. It left every train ride and time in a city center with a heightened level of alertness. I looked over my shoulder more often than before. Turns out one of my London coworkers had been at the site of the bombing in Paris the night before it happened. She was there visiting her boyfriend and out for dinner. That's how close it was.

Jess and I talked it over, wondering if we should keep our plan to visit Paris scheduled for just a week later. When we thought about what we wanted that trip to be, however, we wanted a fun girls' trip, and Paris was a city in mourning covered in heightened police presence. We decided to focus on France but find a new city to enjoy.

As I looked around for spots that were within easy reach of her new German home, we discovered Lyon, a city about four hours by train from her town. European geography is wild because everything is so close. Jess and her family live in the southwest corner of Germany; however, when I visit them, I fly into Switzerland. That airport sits at the intersection of Germany, France, and Switzerland, and when you leave the airport, you choose the exit that will put you into one of those three countries.

Lyon was billed as the "food capital of France." The food capital of France sounded like visiting the Disneyland *inside* of Disneyland, so we were all about it. With travel points and off-season rates, I found us a five-star hotel overlooking the square at the heart of the city. The hotel was situated on a street corner, and in addition to standard hotel rooms, each floor had one unique room that sat on the corner of the building, complete with a rounded corner balcony and three French doors wrapping around the exterior wall and opening onto the balcony outside. The room was the size of a small apartment, covered in toile furnishings, and I could not have felt more French than when we walked into that space.

The bellman opened the balcony doors to show us the night skyline of the plaza below and pointed to the illuminated Notre Dame church on the hill above the city. I was so taken with the magic of that place that I tossed my hands above my head and yelled, "Helloooo Lyon!" (Pro tip, this brash display of American excitement does not seem to be appreciated in French culture, in case you ever find yourself in a similar situation.)

Lyon is a city made of dreams. Their cathedral sits on a hill above Vieux Lyon (Old Lyon), which embodies the essence of old-world Europe with its cobblestone streets, low doorways, and narrow winding paths. There are a few ways to ascend to the church on top of the hill, one being a funicular train that is part of their metro system, which of course we took to the top. Because we wanted to see the cathedral and the view, and because when can you use a Metro card to ride a funicular, right?

Vieux Lyon is bordered by the Saône River, and once over the bridge to the other side, the architecture turns to the Parisian style of white multiple-story buildings with the classic floor-to-ceiling windowed doors opening onto balconies. Always with the doors onto balconies.

On the other side of this center part of the city is the Rhône River, which divides the most modern and contemporary part of Lyon from these two more classically French areas. The Rhône runs south to the Mediterranean Sea, creating a key stop on the Silk Road, historically bringing colorful textiles into France via its waterways. It's a mature and humble city, full of subtle personality, history, and incredible smells and flavors. It was one of the first times in my life that a brand-new foreign city felt like home. The vibe of the people, the well-dressed, yet laid-back, culture, the ease of getting around, the shops, it was all comfortable yet novel. And I felt completely myself.

Every trip during the travel year was sure to include some frivolity and capers. By my second trip to London later that year, the spring weather was emerging, and there was much more opportunity to be outside. I had a friend in grad school there, and one weekend, we took chilled rosé and a picnic to Richmond Park on the outskirts of London. Famous for its sprawling open spaces and population of deer, we found a spot under a tree by the lake to picnic. Lying on a white blanket, reading books, we felt every bit like the ladies of Downton Abbey.

The year also included multiple trips to the East Coast, L.A., and San Francisco. I spent a month in the winter in San Diego, a city very much in the running as my next place to call home. That spring also saw a two-week trip to Japan to meet my new nephew and soak up time with my niece. I'd been there a bunch already, but this was my first trip where the timing perfectly aligned with the emerging cherry blossoms, the sakura. We walked castle grounds with moats surrounded in the pink fireworks of the blossoms and drank warm sake on cushions in parks shaded by blooming trees. The late spring took me back to London for a few weeks, and in the summer, I spent six weeks in the Pacific Northwest exploring both Portland and Seattle as additional relocation options. I had friends or made friends every place I went, so there was always community to be had. I even made new friends on planes, too. One of the biggest lessons I learned on that year of travel is that if I opened my heart and expanded definitions, anywhere can feel like home.

Along with all the fun, each stay had to include the mental and logistical lift of examination and future planning. A year is a long time, and yet it flew by. With an end date, there was no time to waste in scoping out a city that was actually in the running for a future home. I went into the year with a short list of West Coast cities: San Diego, Portland, and Seattle. Really, I was mostly settled on San Diego. Around the second half of the year, though, I started to feel a pull to the East Coast, with its more classically metropolitan cities and proximity to Europe. It was a far-off whisper, one that made no sense based on where I thought I was headed.

With that said, and at the risk of jumping ahead, I am now writing this tale of fernweh adventure from my home in Boston, if that gives you a sense of how loud that little whisper about the East Coast became. Yet another fernweh adventure. Hang tight, I promise to fill in the details.

It's so valuable to truly understand what your fernweh is as you set out on the adventure. By having a vision for the dream you are pursuing, you can pursue it wholeheartedly and you can play with new ideas and options along the way. You can try something on for size without a threat to your mission or character, because you know what those things are.

Many of my friends will tell you that I'm big into "what if?" Not only am I an ideator by nature, which means I'm always thinking of potential new things to try, but I'm also the first one to try an out-of-the-box idea on for size. What if I just tried it, asked the question, lived somewhere else for a month, or a year? The answer can always be no. No is a complete sentence. But the answer will always be no unless we actually ask the question.

As you start to step out on your own fernweh adventure, identify some key things: What is the overall goal of your journey? What are some of the destinations you want to have on your journey because they fold into your overall goal? What are some adventures you want to have, some paths you want to go down simply for the enjoyment of them? What is your own version of frivolity that will make your journey more colorful along the way?

Asking yourself these questions will help you navigate the implementation and enjoyment of your fernweh. And when things get bumpy along the way, as they most assuredly will, they will guide you back to your original purpose. And remember that even as you seek your purpose, and come to understand what you were made for, that there is always fun to be had. You get to delight in this dream of yours, not just live through it.

CHAPTER THIRTEEN

There Will be Risk

There is a Robert Frost quote that I often go back to in challenging times, "The best way out is always through." The truth about the things that make the journey more colorful, more flavorful, more fun, and even more accomplished are that they require risk. This means grappling with the usual cast of risk-averse characters like fear for our safety, fear of loneliness, fear of looking foolish, fear of not being good enough, fear of being judged, fear of being new at something, or even being afraid we won't know where to start.

It also means that at each of these more intimidating intersections, we have the choice to back away from the fernweh path we are on or choose ourselves and our dream. More often than not, what we find on the other side is so much bigger and better than the fear that tried to stand in our way. Before we can realize it, the fear that seemed like a giant stopping our progress becomes tiny in our rearview mirror. But we have to choose for ourselves, not just once, but over and over again. For always.

Anyone who knows me well knows that I am a huge U2 fan. Since I was about twelve years old, they've been my band. I heard them for the first time on a tape copied by two of the cool boys at school and passed on to my best friend, who was crushing on one of them. They may have even been "going together," if that takes you back a minute. She and I were hanging out in her room, probably comparing jelly shoes, when the sounds of the *Joshua Tree* album came out of the boom box on her dresser, and it was pure magic. The song, "Where the Streets Have No Name," was like being transported to another place altogether, and in that moment, I'd found the first music that was purely mine. Free from the influences of my parents' Motown and the social pressure of emulating Madonna. It didn't matter how anyone else felt about them; they were my band, my boys, and my music.

Seeing U2 play live was my first major concert, a weekend adventure with girlfriends in high school, where the Sugarcubes opened, and a cute boy named Eddie asked me to slow dance in the aisle with him on the last song. In all, I've seen U2 in concert thirteen times, in seven cities and three countries. I've read books and articles about the band's history and music, been a member of the fan club, preached a sermon about one of their songs, and waited outside the arena before a show to get autographs. I only have Adam's so far.

So when they were touring Europe during my year of travel, did I *happen* to put those dates on my planning calendar and did

I *possibly* work my time in London to coincide with their tour dates? Uh. Yeah. The show was on a weeknight after work, and I waited to see if anyone would be interested in joining me. Of course, because it's more fun to go with a friend, but also because of some lingering situational anxiety that sort of always sat there on the backburner of my life at that time.

My particular brand of anxiety hits me when I feel like I don't have a way out of situations. Like concert venues and crowds and, oh, also, the city center subway stops one has to go through to get all the way to the other side of London where, say, a large-scale music event might occur.

But of course, my boys were worth it, and there was no way I was not going to see them play in London, another city and another country to add to the growing list of shows. No one was available to come with me, so I found a seat for the show in an unsold group of four just before the end of the workday, printed the ticket, and headed out of the office to go change and catch the Underground, about a forty-minute ride to the venue.

On my walk back to the flat, I popped 'round one of the shops to buy something, only to hear on the radio that there was an incident on the Tube that would redirect thousands of commuters getting home. I asked the shopkeeper what that meant for my journey to the O2 Arena and, in his Cockney accent, one of the true Londoners left in the city, he said, "Aw, yeah, love, you better get goin'. Even leaving now, you might not make it."

My heart sank. I was already struggling with anxiety about getting there, and now this random fluke thing layered on top made it an even bigger challenge. If you've not had this type of anxiety, it's hard to explain. Basically every step forward has to be a conscious decision to get through to the next one. So to turn and leave that shop, to hurry and get going, was a decision I had to remind myself to make. To go home, change clothes, and get out the door, rather than becoming paralyzed and letting the clock run out while I hid at home, was another series of decisions. To leave the house, walk down the street, and especially to enter the bustling Notting Hill Station were all intentional decisions to be made. Getting on the train, another deliberate decision.

The Notting Hill Station is a medium anxiety level of difficulty for me. The platform is not a far distance from either the street level above or the bottom of the stairs below. If I felt the need to flee, I could be out and above ground in probably ninety seconds or less. So while I was cruising along on my emotional obstacle course, it was a soft start out of the gate. Getting into the train car, I chose the empty seat closest to the door and counted the stops along the route to the large central London station where I would need to change trains.

The next line would send me directly into the heart of the city and the redirected commuters, all trying to make their way home on an unfamiliar route with theirs out of service for the night. That next Underground line would also send me two stories farther underneath the city. A quick exit was no longer an option, with even just the escalator ride alone taking minutes. If you haven't yet seen the escalators in central London, they are dizzyingly steep. Not to mention the tunnels to walk between platforms that are measured not in feet or meters but in portions of miles.

I transferred at one of the central stations, finding the Jubilee Line and again choosing the closest seat I could find to the door. At this early point in the journey, there was still some open space in the car. From here, it would be about ten stops under the city, and we would cross under the river three times. I began to live my entire life one subway stop at a time as I managed my anxiety moment by moment.

Each stop took us further into the city, into that night's commuter confusion, and into the crowd of people also headed to the concert. Every time the doors opened, I willed people to get off the train and leave me an open escape route, but alas, with each sliding door, more passengers joined me on the journey. After just a stop or two, all the seats were filled, with many folks standing, holding on to the bars above. A couple more stops and I could no longer see the door from my seat. I pleaded with them in my mind, *Please move. Please get off the train. Please move out of my way.* No one budged.

It's logical to wonder why I didn't just stand up and move closer to the door. However, part of my type of anxiety is that I feel dizzy, sometimes as if vertigo has set in. As you might imagine, that doesn't mix well with standing on a moving train. So I held my ground, or rather, my seat, knowing that if I gave up that seat, I wouldn't find another open one. Each time the doors opened, I was tempted to run for the platform, to get out of that moving tube, out of the subterranean system and back out into the fresh air. Well, fresh air by giant city standards.

I had to decide to stay on that train every time a new opportunity came to leave it. I chose to stay. Chose to keep moving forward, toward this thing that I'd been dreaming of and planned part of my trip around. But it wasn't just about choosing to see a concert. It was about choosing myself. Every single time those doors closed and the train started to move on to the next stop, I'd chosen myself. And I'd have to do it again in another mile or two. And I did. I chose myself and who I wanted to be all across the city of London that night.

The Jubilee Line delivered me to North Greenwich Station, right on the doorstep of the O2 Arena. I'd purchased a special section seat, so it had its own entrance, which made the experience feel all the more worthwhile once I arrived at the venue. I found my seat, and it turned out the three empties around me had also been scooped up by solo concert goers. The man to my left was from Ireland, just like the band, and U2 was also his favorite group. He was a good head taller than me. I barely came up to his shoulder. In the middle of the show, when my boys started to play, "Where the Streets Have No Name," we all jumped to our feet, and my seatmate threw his arms around with such vigorous excitement that his elbow came crashing down onto my head. He didn't even notice that he'd elbowed me in the skull like a pro wrestler. The funniest part to me is that instead of being mad, I thought to myself, *Me too, dude, me too.*

My heart was full, of course, from seeing this band I'd grown up with on their side of the world, but mostly because of how far God had brought me. Across the city, across the ocean, and across the desert of emotional and mental emptiness to get to this adventure in the first place.

Going after the things that make you happy, that make your heart sing, that help you feel alive, will scare you. They will require risk. You will be forced to adapt on the fly, to take a path that makes you uncomfortable, and to find a redirected route at times. If you don't experience these things, I might suggest again that you're not risking big enough. And keep in mind, your risk will look different than mine. But it will be big for you. And it will be worth choosing yourself at every stop.

CHAPTER FOURTEEN

The Small Things are the Big Things

This feels like a good place to demystify some things about fernweh, starting with the reality that often it's actually about the little things. When we're pursuing a lofty goal, a big adventure, a more fulfilling life, it's easy to think that the point of the journey are those big moments, the pinch me, "I can't believe this is real life and I'm actually here doing this" moments. Don't get me wrong, following your fernweh definitely comes with those. And, oh my gosh, are they fun. They are magic, like we saw already.

But here's the straight talk. If what you are pursuing is the fernweh in your heart, calling you from far away, you will revel in the small, simple things about it, too. Even the things that seem mundane or irritating. For example, I came to love packing for a trip, even though I did it about every three weeks. Of course, you will also be annoyed by some of the mundane things. Just like in your regular life. Because the thing is, following your fernweh is going to *become* part of your regular life, if you let it. But we'll get to that later.

Before I left for London the first time, I was struggling with what coat to take. Being a Californian, I didn't have the proper outerwear for that part of the world, and then there is the fashion sense of Europe to consider. Living in Silicon Valley, people wear jeans and tees with sneaks or flips. When it's cold, you might see a North Face jacket, so it's not exactly an area famous for its posh city wear. A friend suggested buying a coat once I arrived in Europe. Less to carry, great souvenir, treat myself. Sold. Done and done.

On the first night of my trip to Edinburgh, I found the perfect wool coat. Light gray, wraparound with tie-waist style, and a large floppy collar that can lay flat on the shoulders or pop up around the ears and neck. Not only did I find the coat, but a pair of cute ankle boots as well. I took my new treasures back to my hotel and changed to go out for the night.

So where does one start for a first evening out in Scotland? With Scotch, of course. As with many European cities, the city center hub is the train station. Also true for Edinburgh, with the added luxury of the five-star Balmoral Hotel atop the station. Not only is this spot home to a Michelin-rated restaurant, it also has Scotch, a bar dedicated to their specialty spirit and offering over five hundred options of whiskey. That was my first stop of the night, and it was what you'd imagine: low lighting, dark woods, brown and gold decor accents, and lots of leather, including a leather-bound book housing the drink menu. The servers wore vests and ties with a kilt, and brought a love and expertise of whiskey that helped a novice like me find my perfect match.

I was seated against the wall in a velvety armchair, warm light from the lamp on the side table next to me and a view of the bar so I could appropriately eavesdrop and people watch. When the server brought my selection, an Aberlour 16 in a Glencairn whiskey glass, it was on a leather tray with a side of chocolate-covered almonds and a water back. It remains to this day one of my top five drinks of all time. Sitting there, I was very aware that I was in a bar alone, and it took work to resist the urge to rush the experience and, instead, center myself on being fully present in the moment. I sipped from the glass, ate the almonds one by one slowly and intentionally, and took the time to read the stories of whiskey in the leather-bound drink menu and just *be*. When I'd finished my scotch and saturated my soul in the space, I stood up, put on my new coat, tying it at the waist, and walked out into the crisp night air.

Now, one hot tip for gals traveling alone: know where you are going before you leave your current location. I almost always have my destination pulled up on the phone map, knowing the next turn before I get there, so there is no pausing at intersections and corners. You want to walk with intentionality and carry yourself like you own that space. If you have to look at the map on your phone, act like you're texting rather than looking at directions.

So, knowing where I was going, I tucked my hands into the pockets of my smart new coat and listened to the sound of my new boots clicking down the sidewalk as I headed quickly for my next stop. One of my greatest joys of that trip, and to this day the thing that makes me feel like a gal about town, is the sound of my own boots on a city street. I feel empowered and free simultaneously, simply with the small clack of my heels hitting the ground. That night in Edinburgh, I was on a weekend trip away from my London "home," not actually home to me at all. I was both scared and I was liberated, knowing this was another moment encapsulating everything that the dreaming and preparation for the months before had brought me.

As I rounded a corner, a woman, perhaps the age of my mother, said, "Excuse me," in her Scottish accent, and then asked me for directions. She seemed surprised to hear my American accent tell her I was just visiting Edinburgh and didn't know the city. It felt like I had arrived, blending in like a local, which had been part of my wish for that year, to move through cities like a local. That was one of my favorite nights of the entire year of travel.

So, let's recap what happened: I bought a coat, had a drink, and a woman asked me for directions. Nothing glamorous or even noteworthy at all. At least, not on their own. When you pay attention to the small moments, however, and savor the sounds, smells, and flavors, a simple event will begin to tell a story and remind you why you are pursuing this adventure. If you are on your fernweh path, the small things will be just as grand to you as the big things.

From then on, after that trip to Scotland, I walked to work each morning, hearing the tapping of my heels on the London streets, my smart coat tied at the waist, surrounded by the city and the absolute glee of not wanting to be anywhere else in the world.

Let's take this out of the travel realm for a moment and focus on something closer to home, like literally at home. Being a parent. People feel all kinds of ways about becoming a parent prior to actually doing it. For some folks, it's a terrifying proposition they come to accept slowly. For others, raising a family is their fernweh. For the latter, it is the drumbeat deep within their heart, calling to them, the purpose they know they are meant to pursue. Recently, I talked with a dear friend who could have chosen a lot of paths—medicine, education, or faith-based work—but her dream was to be a mom. Not just any mom, but the kind of mom who is on the floor, playing in the mud, choosing moments together with intention, and pointing her children toward strong character and faith.

She was always going to be amazing at it. She's the kind of person who can make a picnic from the best the convenience store has to offer and win a Halloween costume contest with what she finds in the back of her closet. She cares deeply, loves well, laughs a lot, and learns as she goes. At the moment, she's got four little ones all under the age of seven, and I asked her about what it's like to be in the middle of her fernweh journey as a parent. She's not dreaming about it anymore, it's not a faraway thought, and she's also not coming to the end of it; there are literally decades to go. She is planted directly in the middle of four little lifetimes of fernweh adventure.

She shared about how, prior to becoming a parent, there was an idealism about the way it was all going to go. She had every intention of homeschooling them all, and while that plays out well for some families, she let go of the idea of being her children's teacher in favor of other priorities for their family. She spoke about the levels of exhaustion, frustration, and lessons in humility she didn't even know were possible until parenthood, and yet how the delight in the small and day-to-day things was the actual journey itself. How she loves to watch them light up in discovery of the world as she teaches them and is the primary witness to them experiencing all life has to offer for the first time.

She told me of recently taking them on a fishing day to a local lake. The outing turned into a windy mess of trying to find shelter and pretty much skipping out on fishing altogether. As her husband and her oldest ventured out to find a less windy casting spot, she stayed behind with the two-week-old snuggled against her chest in the carrier, watching Two and Three run from her to the water and back, over and over again. They didn't mind about the wind, or the lack of actual fishing. They were in the moment, playing together.

My dear friend has come to find that her fernweh journey as a mom is about the small things that make up the path. She said, "Every small thing we do matters to them, and it matters to God." Her adventure and her contentment have come to live in that space of little moments. She shared a Bible verse with me that she has kept in her children's crib since the first baby was born, from Zechariah 4:10. It says, "Do not despise these small beginnings, for the Lord rejoices to see the work begin." This verse helps her to remember to appreciate the small things, be proud of the sometimes mundane and frustrating moments, and remember that her journey is made up of many small stepping stones throughout each day that create a massive path for her little ones to grow on. Every day does not feel like a victory, but when she looks back over their lives, the little events add up to their big story.

I also happen to believe the small things you enjoy in life can help you reverse engineer what your fernweh might be and how to prioritize what you focus on. The experiences you love, want to share with others, could soak in all day—those are the hallmarks of the particular brand of adventure that fills your spirit. If you are still struggling to identify or define your personal fernweh, spend a bit thinking about your simple pleasures. What small moments make your heart sing? What experiences, done alone or shared with others, fill your heart up? What places or things do you want to share with others so they can see how wonderful they are, too?

These small moments might be the start of a journey for you, the beginning of a thing that you love, that starts your engine or keeps you going. They might also be the moments you want to prioritize along the path—to make sure they happen, to ensure they are part of your fernweh adventure. There will be big moments, magic, grand firework displays to be in awe of. The small moments, however, are the glitter that make simple things feel special and celebrated. Watch for that glitter; it's everywhere.

CHAPTER FIFTEEN

A Lot of it is a Slog

When we think of someone pursuing their passions, what comes to mind might be the pictures, the highlight reel of their mountaintops, shared in social posts or holiday cards. Is that a bad thing? Of course not. Is it human nature to want to put our best face forward and to share the best of ourselves? Sure. But speaking for myself, I only feel like sharing when it's going well. When I'm struggling, I turn inward and become more quiet. So the lack of *real* shared experiences may also be self-preservation and self-conservation, not a lack of those hard moments happening at all.

We have to remember that every person following their fernweh has so many more boring and hard moments than they do the mountaintop moments. As I wrote these lines, a work colleague was just days away from her first ever bikini fitness competition.

She posted amazing before and after pictures of her strength and her muscle definition and wrote, "I will not say the whole journey has been easy. There have been days when I had to fight myself to go to the gym or stick to my meal plan, but I won those battles every time!"

In her first competition, she won four medals, including two first-place spots on the podium. The first thing she did off stage was shove a mini red velvet Bundt cake in her mouth as fast as she could. Then, where was she Monday morning at 4:30 a.m.? Right back at the weights rack, headphones in, ready to tackle her next challenge and prepare for the next competition. It's not all hair extensions and spray tans, people. It's putting in the reps, celebrating our small wins, and using our story to encourage others.

My college roommate, Taylor, is one of my best personal examples of not giving up when the obstacles and the weight of the journey seem insurmountable. I met Taylor when she was two years into college; we both rented rooms in this pit of an apartment half a block from the beach in Southern California. Taylor was back at school after having taken some time off for a mental health crisis. She'd been in the biology program at one of the most competitive pre-med programs in the state when a hallucinogenic episode occurred, sending her plans off track. She was ambitious, dreaming of becoming a doctor since childhood, knowing that a helping field would be her purpose, and suddenly she was halted in place on that path.

She began to deal with crippling anxiety and panic disorder, as her logical brain, her fierce independence, and her physiological symptoms were now constantly at war. When I met her, it had come to a place where she could not function well in daily life and her medical provider prescribed an anti-anxiety medication. Taylor had determined for herself that she would never take a substance, as that had been the inciting cause of the hallucinogenic episode that started her down this path a few years earlier. However, she was now years into this battle and had run out of non-medicinal options. As a devout Catholic, she struggled profoundly with what using medication meant about the fortitude of her faith. If she'd only had more faith, trusted God more, would she not need the help of science? If only she'd never experimented with substances in the first place. If only counseling was working better. All the *what ifs* and *if onlys* swirled around uninvited.

When she made the decision to take her first anti-anxiety dose, Taylor, her best friend, and I sat around the kitchen table with a small round blue pill sitting on the tabletop in front of us. We listened as she lamented and grieved what had brought her to this place. Her emotions, will, and logic wrestled with one another in resistance and stubbornness while tears streamed down her face. She held on to what would have and should have been, knowing desperately that this solution could be the start of a new hope for the future. We listened and reasoned together for hours, not knowing if she'd be able to take that first dose as the night went on. And then, she did it. She put that miniscule and momentous blue dot in her mouth and swallowed. A tiny and monumental step in her journey. Like standing on the edge of a cliff, picking up a foot, and just leaning forward and letting yourself fall. She had taken that giant fall into the unknown.

After the trauma of her early years at college, Taylor stepped away from pre-med and chose a liberal arts path, eventually becoming a middle school teacher. Not one prone to anything basic, with an ever-humming internal engine driving her to more, she earned her teaching credential and a master's degree in creative writing during the summers. She taught special education at a middle school for emotionally disturbed children. My petite five-foot-one friend found herself in a space with emerging adults sometimes prone to throwing objects, including furniture. She never balked at any of this. Instead, what gnawed at her was the far-off dream of medicine. That dream still lingered there, like a wind chime on the corner of a house, sometimes still, sometimes clanging when the weather kicked up.

By this time we weren't living in the same city, and our regular phone catch-ups on our after-work commutes consistently included some mention of medical school. Over a few years of these calls, she bought herself a home, adopted a huge goofy dog named Casey, got married, did home improvement projects, and wrote stories in her free time. It was a great life, but it wasn't whole. Not for her.

If you've ever been in proximity to someone going through medical school, you know that it is a long and arduous journey, which is often why if someone hasn't started it within a year or two of undergrad, it's off the table. That practical timeline, coupled with our cultural expectations about age, second careers, and so on, means considering medical school past the mid-twenties is rare. Taylor had all these doubts present, which helped her to drown out that ever so faint drumbeat of a career in medicine. She tried to sublimate her desire to help and serve others through her educational career, volunteer work, personal interests, and family life. And yet, that drumbeat lingered in the background, becoming gradually louder until finally she let herself acknowledge that it was there.

Once she admitted she was still dreaming of a career in medicine, she gave herself permission to research what her options would be for entering medical school with a non-traditional path to its door. Then she committed to studying for the MCAT and applying and interviewing for schools. Then she got accepted. All while maintaining her full-time teaching career, being a relative newlywed, and, oh, having her first baby.

At thirty-one, while still nursing her son, this determined, feisty, and moderately terrified woman began her medical school career. She knew early on that she wanted to focus on mental health to help others who have struggled and suffered as she had. There were massive wins along the way, and struggles, too. She had to learn to advocate for herself, to battle the insecurity of being the "older" student, and to balance home life with this pursuit of her dream. But what was no longer lingering around every corner was this sense that she was somehow missing out on something. She was squarely in the sweet spot of the "something" that had been calling to her from childhood. She was not only hearing that drumbeat from deep in her soul, she was learning to play in time with it.

I'm going to fast-forward the full nine-year process and let you know that she finished four years of school, becoming Dr. Taylor. Then she completed four years of a psychiatry residency, and then an additional year of a fellowship focused on a specialty with children and adolescents. Also, during that time, she and her husband welcomed three more boys into their family, which meant three family leaves away from medical school. Three chances to reconsider her dream and step away from it. But she didn't. She followed her fernweh, however long that road had to be, with its switchbacks and rocks and rushing rivers.

What are some of the best things I've learned from watching my friend follow her fernweh?

- It is never too late.
- A lot of it is a slog.
- We can live a full life in tandem with following our own internal call.
- The journey might be long, full of complicated steps and even some falls.
- We can be scared, insecure, and inexperienced and do it anyway.
- We can be in over our head and learn to swim.

Who in your life has followed their fernweh on a journey that took years? What do you notice about that experience for them? Were they growing as a person? Were they thriving? Where did they become weary? Did you support them when they did?

From the outside looking in, it feels like the training, schooling, and personal and professional goals of others fly by. A friend tells us they are thinking of going to school for something, and before we know it, we are celebrating their graduation. Time is going to pass by quickly no matter what. We can spend it doubting, stalling, waiting, overthinking, sublimating, and being distracted. Or we can choose to stare that dream right in the face, understanding that it will always be with us, and make the choice to learn its rhythm and dance with it. Time will pass no matter what. The choice becomes about where and how you will spend that precious time.

I would love to tell you that my friend "made it," but that's not how fernweh works. In the passion Taylor is pursuing, there is always more to learn, more to try, more adventure to be had. But she has discovered the land of her personal style of adventure, and the looming sense that there is a more fulfilling alternate path that she missed out on has been eliminated. She has chosen that path, her dream, her fernweh. The doubt and the wondering *what if?* and *if only* are gone. Her courage and grit inspire me, but not because she's a doctor. Taylor inspires me because she battled for her life at a kitchen table, clutching a glass of water and the hope for a better future all those years ago.

CHAPTER SIXTEEN

There Will Still be Heartbreak

You would think that the hardest part of pursuing your dreams is the getting going. But even as you pursue your dreams right on the edge, toes on the line, everything feeling intentional and deliberate and magical, life goes on. Hardships and heartbreak still happen. This is absolutely true, even in the perfect pocket of your fernweh pursuit.

The second half of my year of fernweh brought even more adventures. I lived in San Diego for a month and in the Pacific Northwest for most of the summer, both explorative times to see about living in those regions full-time. I visited my brother and his family in Japan, and I went back to Europe, first to London for work and then to Germany again to see Ben and Jess.

By now, you can probably sense that one of the details where God shows off in my life is through timing. When I lived in San Diego, I rented a room through a friend of a friend called Jordan. On that second trip to London, a few months after staying with Jordan in San Diego, she happened to be coming through the U.K. on her way back from an extended trip to see family overseas. So she came to stay with me, seeing London during the day on her own and then we would go out at night. We had a couple fun evenings in the city where we saw Harrods, we flirted with British military blokes, part of the Queen's equestrian brigade, and we crushed it with two other Americans at pub trivia.

Even with the fun of having a friend there, that trip to London was much different than the first one. Months had passed, and a lifetime of changes had come. I stayed in a different neighborhood than before—this time, instead of a lovely walk, my commute was a Tube or bus ride to Notting Hill Station. The bus took longer on the surface streets than the Underground would have, but I loved the romance of riding the red London buses through the gorgeous roads of Kensington, one route taking me right past Kensington Palace. I would peek through the gates, seeing the cars and security, and wonder what Kate and Wills were up to.

It was coming on spring at that point, and the winter had been tough. Of course, I brought my boots back with me and still loved the sound of my heels clicking on the street, but they were some-how harder to hear. The joy of that sound had dulled a bit. The last time I'd been there, James and I were just getting started in our romance, and often as I walked home from work, a message would pop up from him and we would pick up getting to know each other from the day before, all the questions, ideas, compliments, and flirtations. On this second trip to London, there were no messages. A few months before, still soaking in the bliss of the hard-to-find connection we had, we also realized that our practical lives didn't fit together. Where we were each headed, how we lived our lives, and what we saw for our future didn't match up. So we came to the heartbreaking place of letting each other go. Even though the weather was cheerier than my last time in London, the city somehow felt grayer than before.

Around the same time of saying goodbye to this hope of love with James, one of my closest friendships fell apart. I'd had a dear friend of almost fifteen years come to a place of dramatic change in her own life. This change caused an incredible amount of hurt across many of her relationships, including ours. We'd met in a Bible study that she'd invited herself to, as she was always one who wanted to both welcome others and to be welcomed herself. She was full of laughter and self-effacing humor, and we connected instantly.

She was a friend I'd traveled with, cried with, and howled in laughter with. I was in the recovery room when her son was born through cesarean in the middle of the night, meeting him even before his grandparents did. Both her children called me Auntie. We were each other's go-to for every event, the friends who check in about what we're wearing and coordinated getting there together, often with a sleepover at one of our houses after. She took me to doctor's appointments when I was nervous, and I took her kids and her cat for overnights and weekends. She was one of my closest friends, much more like family than just a friend, and she was gone with a phone call and an email.

And then there was Liz.

Our Lizzie, who was five foot one and larger than life. Liz was a cheerleader in high school and in personality, a teacher by trade, and a soul singer at heart. She was the girl that no matter how impractical, would rock hot pink acrylic nails and five-inch stilettos. She would give a piece of her mind to linebacker-sized fellas if she thought they looked at her friend sideways. She was the first one on the dance floor, with her arms in the air and her eyes closed, savoring every beat and sway. She carried the love, grace, and embrace of the Spirit of God within her. She was the friend that no matter how big your mistake or how ridiculously you embarrassed yourself, she would love you with her whole heart, never judge you, help you to pick yourself up, dust off your knees, and get back out there.

And as I was in London for a second adventure, she was back home dying of cancer.

A few months earlier, Liz, who was newly engaged to a pillar of a man named Ed—having found that once-in-a-lifetime love, the stuff epic cinematic love stories are made of—started having pain in her abdomen. A trip to the ER led to surgery, which led to a diagnosis, which led to chemo. Things progressed much too quickly, and while they'd originally planned a fall wedding in a beautiful barn venue, a few months after her cancer journey began, a group of us gathered in the backyard of her mother-in-law's house to celebrate as she and Ed, her great love, were married. Liz hadn't been able to even get out of bed in the days before the wedding, and yet, on that day, she was able to dance, with her arms in the air and her eyes closed, a white and purple flower crown in her hair. That is how I picture our gorgeous girl in heaven now.

Shortly after returning from London, the time came to see her and say goodbye. In God's sweet timing yet again, I was able to delay a trip and sit with her for a day, just the two of us. We said all the things that needed to be said, and about a week later, the call came on a Friday morning as I was in a line in a new city to buy pastries for the office. She was gone.

Here's the thing. That year of travel was equally one of the best and the hardest years of my life. I was more bold and brave than I'd ever been. Ever. And yet, I experienced some of the most heartbreaking losses I'd ever had. I don't think it was an accident this all happened at the same time. That's the thing about life. It's not meant to be lived in the average, in the mean. When we have the highs, we are meant to celebrate and savor them. And when we have loss, we are meant to feel it, to let it do its work in our hearts and spirits. I don't mean that we get stuck there, but that we allow the losses on our journey to be part of who we are, part of our story.

This is all the more reason to go after your fernweh. Like, right now, friend. There will always be hard things. There will always be something to derail you. You don't have to set it to the side to pursue your drumbeat; it can all be together, woven into the story that you are telling with your life. Honor the heartbreak; give it the space it needs to be felt and to heal. But don't let it stop you, sidetrack you, or cause you to sit down on the path and set up camp there. That is not what you were made for. And at the risk of being cliché, the Liz of my life, and whoever the Liz is in your life, would never want that for us.

They would want us to keep fighting, keep chasing, and keep dreaming.

I remind myself of this often. When Liz died, I made a promise to her and to myself that I would do my best to follow her example of being the first one on the dance floor. Oh, and to always order the guacamole. And how little did I know that I would need that reminder of courage and risk much sooner than I could imagine.

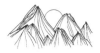

Summary: Enjoy Steps

- There will be magic, and you deserve to enjoy it richly.
- Take risk and choose yourself. Again and again. You are worth it.
- Watch for the small things; they are actually the big things.
- Keep going.
- Know there will be heartbreak. It's part of the journey.

PART 4

Guard Your Fernweh

CHAPTER SEVENTEEN

Keep Your Wits About You

Even though you are chasing a lofty dream, remember to keep yourself grounded and to keep your wits about you. Whether you are traveling, starting school or a business, leaning into philanthropic work, whatever it is, there are everyday practical pitfalls, and there are pits you can fall into specific to what you choose to pursue. Not everything is lofty. You still need to read the fine print, be aware of your surroundings, and keep your head up.

When I was in Scotland, I headed to dinner at a restaurant that had great reviews. While the restaurant itself seemed warm and inviting in the photos, as I turned down the street it was on, it quickly became a dark cobblestone side street. Suddenly, the sound of my smart boots clicking down the road lost its fun. I became acutely aware of being alone in a foreign city, and as I got just a couple of shop lengths away from the main street, a man chatted me up from the other side of this narrow way. I deflected, turned on my heels, and headed for the more populated main road. Great reviews or otherwise, it wasn't worth it. Even when chasing our fernweh, we still must listen to that feeling in our gut that tells us to abandon ship.

In another situation late in the fernweh year, I'd had a lengthy trip going from two weeks in London to a weekend in Germany, to a work stopover in New York, to a weekend in Washington, D.C. After almost three weeks of travel in three countries, my suitcase was bulging at the seams, and when I boarded the Acela Express train from Manhattan to D.C., I was lucky to find an empty spot in the luggage rack with a seat just nearby so I could keep an eye on my bag.

The route was dotted with stops across several states, with most stations being simple roadside platforms. At each stop, the train allowed just a few minutes of transition time as passengers exited and entered the cars. Somewhere in the middle of the ride, as the train slowed to a stop and passengers began to exit the car, I heard a large crash in the luggage box and looked to see a baby stroller drop to the floor where my suitcase had been. Looking into the aisle, I saw a man carrying my bag towards the door of the train car. I verbally tried to get his attention, to no avail. In a matter of moments, all my clothes for the rest of the trip and all my treasures collected from weeks in Europe and a stop in New York were about to disappear out that door and into a city that I would be carried away from as the train moved on.

Just as he made the left turn from the center aisle into the threshold space of the exit door, I grabbed the handle on the top of his backpack and jerked him back. "You're taking my suitcase!" I yelled. He stepped back, set my suitcase down in front of me, feigned as though he'd mistakenly picked up the wrong bag, and left the train.

Not to dramatically lean into this metaphor, but y'all, people will try to walk off with your goods on this journey. Do not let them. Hold your boundaries, say no, take back your treasures, your space, your voice, whatever has been grabbed. It is not theirs; they have no right to touch it, much less walk off with it. Get bold. Get help if you need to.

CHAPTER EIGHTEEN

Know Your Worth

While following your fernweh may start out as a small spark of interest for you, there are some fernweh journeys that grow into something bigger, like a business or a career. Which also means somewhere along the line it morphs from hobby to an income-generating endeavor. If this is part of your fernweh dream, and plan, then get serious about it. Find mentors, invest in business tools, and learn what people in that industry are doing. This also means understanding the economics of it, including what you, your talent, experience, service, product, and time should be valued at.

In short, if your fernweh is something you want to get paid for, then get paid what you're worth. Don't second-guess it. Don't apologize for it. Ask for a rate or a price that matches your skill and product level, and don't look back.

I have a friend who runs his own business, part of which includes being hired to speak at events. As his skill developed and his name recognition grew, his booking calendar became so full that he was feeling it carve into time with his family. He had been considering raising his rates for a while but was nervous to outprice his large accounts and sacrifice new business that may come in. At some point, he went for it and later told me that not only was he able to be home with his family more, but his booking request volume increased. As he has repeated this rate increase process additional times, the caliber and visibility of his opportunities has also grown. What he thought would set him back only helped him level up.

Please also note the part I said about his skill developing. We can't come right out of the gate into a new field and charge expert-level rates. I have a friend starting a consulting business who is trying to break into an industry where she has little experience and fewer contacts. Her business mentor has advised her to offer a few companies some free hours of consulting, prove what she can do, gather some learnings for herself, and begin to build her referral network. Even though she's working without monetary exchange, the payoff she will receive could be priceless. It is okay to take a lower rate when it serves to build your long-term goals.

Once your skill is ready for the next level, ask for what you are worth, confidently, head held high, and don't break eye contact. You have nothing to apologize for, nothing to qualify. That is your rate. You are a seasoned professional, and you can expect to be paid as such. I recently saw a quote on Twitter where someone said:

If I do a job in 30 minutes it's because I spent 10 years learning how to do that job in 30 minutes. You owe me for the years, not the minutes.

@davygreenberg

I have a dear college friend who started as a graphic artist, then became the creative and marketing director for a nationwide book, music, and gift distributor. She planned photo shoots, catalog and website designs, and seasonal campaigns. For the next act of her career, she stepped into the entrepreneur life of wedding photography. She is top of her game in her region, continues to take coursework to hone her abilities and stay current with technology and trends, and people travel from across the state to have access to her skill and style. She's also one of the sweetest and kindest people you will ever meet.

Recently, she received a call from the mother of one of her brides trying to negotiate a lower rate, without her daughter knowing this conversation was happening. The couple had chosen my friend's top package, so there was a significant cost. What I love about this friend is, despite her big heart, she values herself as an artist and a businesswoman. So she let the mother know that first, she would need to speak with the daughter, who is the client who contracted with her. She also let the mother know that what she could offer would be to change the package to one of the other price point options, or if they needed to cancel, she understood but would still keep the deposit, as per the contract.

My friend showed she appreciated the tough spot they were in. However, what she did not do was undervalue herself in the process. If you want to make a professional career from your fernweh, at some point you must do this. Otherwise, it's just a hobby.

In a similar vein, please do not feel pressured or obligated to offer discounts on your products and services to people you know. I have seen too many times an expectation that someone sing at a wedding, give a haircut, act as a lawyer or real estate agent, or give handcrafted artisan items all for a discount. Or sometimes for free. If someone values your skill, they will pay you for it. If you would like to offer a gift, that is absolutely your choice and quite generous of you. But it should not be expected. Don't be on the receiving end of that, and don't expect it from others.

Know what you're worth, and ask for it. Still struggling with this idea? Find someone who gets it, who lives it, and learn from their expertise. Just ask what their consulting rate is first, and be ready to pay it.

CHAPTER NINETEEN

Guard Your Fernweh

Recently, I saw a quote from a woman who quit a mainstream corporate job to pursue an online social media business. People who knew her well doubted her decision and questioned her judgement. They expressed concern over how she would make it and where she would be when she failed. However, within two years, she built a four-million-dollar-revenue business and bought her dream car along with a multimillion-dollar home. What was her response when dealing with naysayers?

Never take advice from people who don't have what you want.

@VanessaLau

This is where we need to get real about trust, boundaries, and relationships for a moment. We all have people in our lives, who we love dearly, but who cannot be trusted with this dream right now.

Yep, that person you just thought of. Them.

And it is totally okay. It is not commentary on their value in our lives. You are chasing a dream and pursuing a goal that not everyone will understand. If you were an Olympic-level gymnast, how much could you talk about your training regimen with your great aunt in a way that is relevant and valuable to you achieving your goals? Unless your auntie is a gold medalist, then, by all means, sit at her feet and soak it all in; she knows her stuff.

But if someone is going to throw cold water on this fresh little fire you are kindling (pun absolutely intended), then don't let them into this aspect of your life. Not yet anyway. Wait to tell them about it until you know more clearly what it is and what it's becoming. One of my friends, an artist, was seeing some success in her chosen medium and expressed to her friends how she wanted to take it to the next step and sell her pieces. Her friends teased her about it. Y'all, they teased her. In mocking her, they made it loud and clear they are not the ones to trust with these precious beginnings of her dream. Keep in mind who to trust and who to invest your time with, as that will mean time away from growing on your journey.

This is also where I would encourage you to be open to expanding your circle a bit to people who will understand this crazy dream you've got brewing. I have a friend like this. She is not someone in my everyday inner circle. We used to work together and now see each other about once a year to catch up. She is also a creative who is near the beginning of her fernweh journey. She is pursuing something that may not make sense to everyone, but I see her and get it completely.

A few years back, during a prayer time with God, he gave her the idea to start baking a loaf of bread each week, then pray about who to gift it to and take it to them. So she started baking. Part of the rhythm of her particular drumbeat was to blog about some of the loaves she made and why she felt compelled to share that week's loaf with that specific person. So she started there, including giving her baking project a name. Then she had a special stamp designed with the name of her project along with a Bible verse. She wrapped the bread in a dish towel and tied a tag stamped with her project name on the loaves she gave away. Then she was asked to write an article for an online magazine. Recently, they asked her to start doing Instagram Live cooking segments. Each thing has been something that has pushed her out of her comfort zone. And each one has built her confidence and helped her be ready for the next thing. She's leveling up with each new opportunity.

So when I committed to the big, scary task of writing this book, she was one of the first people I told. It was important to me to have someone in the midst of chasing her own fernweh to be on my cheering squad. I also knew that because she was pursuing her own fernweh, she understood. I knew my dream was safe in her hands. She had stewarded her own dream with honor and purpose. She would do the same for mine because she gets it.

My bread-baking friend is the kind of fellow dreamer to look for and let into your dream. I'm lucky in that each time my fernweh drum has started to beat loud, I have a powerful squad of folks who I can let into the circle. For you, it might be one person; it might be ten. As with all of this, there is no formula. You write the story of your own fernweh journey. As such, do not feel guilty or obligated to let someone into this space in your life. They can be part of it when you let loose whatever this is into the world. While you are nurturing it and growing it, be sure to protect it. It needs light, water, and good food. There is plenty of time for wind, rain, and the negative elements. For now, focus on those who will help you tend and grow it.

If you don't have anyone in your circle currently who is on a similar journey, that's okay. There is nothing wrong with you or your crew. We are all uniquely made, which means the variety of the humans in our lives should be grand. It also may mean that you need to work a little bit to find some like-minded folks. Practically speaking, you can start by looking for shared interest groups in your community or on social media platforms. I know, I know, it can be tough to walk into a new space, physically or virtually. But those groups exist so people with similar interests and passions can gather and share ideas. You have amazing things to add to the conversation and the community. If you try a few and they don't fit, keep looking. Eleanor Roosevelt said:

> Great minds discuss ideas;
> Average minds discuss events;
> Small minds discuss people.

Your people are out there, and they will want to share ideas about your journey, and they will help you grow and change. They are waiting for how you will enrich their journey, too.

Now, before we leave this idea of how to guard your fernweh and who you need with you, there is one more vital group in addition to your fellow gardeners that you need to identify for yourself as you follow your fernweh. You need a cheering squad.

CHAPTER TWENTY

Get You a Cheering Squad

There is a verse in the Bible that says, "Therefore encourage one another and build each other up, just as in fact you are doing" (1 Thessalonians 5:11). There may not be a time when this encouragement from Paul, the writer of this letter, is more relevant than in the pursuit of fernweh. It's a reminder that we are going to have days where self-doubt creeps in, or even roars at us. We're going to have milestones we want to celebrate. You may even be someone who wants an audience to be there when you do the thing. I know that's me at times. I need my people there to celebrate with me.

First, don't underestimate how much celebrating is an important and authentic part of your journey. It's not just about the work or the purpose you are going after; it's about how it changes and grows you as a whole being. It's about the milestones. Let yourself be fully present for this as well. Next, don't do this alone. As we just talked about, you've got to be mindful of who you invite into your journey, but you do want to invite some folks in. I believe it's important to have folks who add fuel to your fire, who build you up, who are in your corner and have your back no matter what.

For me personally, I haven't understood how valuable this cheering squad is until recently, and I'm still learning to embrace it. I struggle with pride and vulnerability. I don't want to be fussed over, or be a burden to a friend on the hard days. But what I'm learning is that to let people in, to let them help us and celebrate us, actually deepens the bonds in relationships. Which takes the fernweh journey beyond just the vertical of the things we are pursuing, but leaves space for the horizontal of encouraging, building up, and building community. And then the journey becomes even sweeter.

One of the best examples of this in my own life is my friend Caelie. I never really understood the phrase "ride or die" until Caelie and I became friends. Whatever the adventure is, Caelie is up for it. She is the kind of friend that if you say, "Hey, let's road trip this weekend," she's got the car packed in ten minutes. She is fiercely loyal and a protector, whether from external influences or internal self-dialogue.

Because Caelie is equipped with a strong sense of self, when I struggle with self-doubt, she is somehow able to just brush it off the table with a "that's nonsense" response, yet without being dismissive of the emotions. She laughs easily, freaks out in all caps and technicolor when I accomplish even small milestones, and looks forward to the good stuff that's coming right alongside me.

She believes in my potential and reminds me to hold on to hope when potential feels far away. She knows the song in my heart and doesn't just sing it, she yells it. Caelie is the ultimate hype girl, and I am so grateful to have her in that role on my journey.

Think for a second if you have a hype girl or guy on your adventure with you. Are you inviting the people in your cheering squad to be part of the experience, or resisting the urge to be vulnerable and celebrated? Equally as important, are you giving back to them, and not just receiving?

You also need folks, even just one, who will show up. On your journey, you need someone who you can ask, "Will you be there?" and you already know the answer. I always know the answer with Steve, a friend of almost twenty years. Steve and I have a depth to our relationship where we call each other out on our garbage, laugh hysterically about silly things, apologize quickly, get over things even quicker, and know what the other one will need or say sometimes even before they do.

With all this depth, Steve can also bring the celebratory fun. For many birthdays, he has shown up with flowers and cake in hand, ready to step in as host and bartender for everyone in attendance. He makes sure folks are fed, happy, and having a great time. More importantly, he makes every celebration feel like a true sense of occasion. He is human confetti.

Steve is also an incredible vocalist and one-half of a music duo, so he understands to his core what it is to have your people show up and cheer for you. And he gives the same back. In the year of a global pandemic, when the world shut down, one of my favorites of these Steve moments happened.

As everything went virtual, many artists had to expand their creativity and adapt their mediums to continue to work. One of my all-time favorite artists, a photographer named Jeremy Cowart, was one of the best innovators in a time that I see as becoming an artistic renaissance. In regular times, Jeremy focuses on commercial work, including images for artists' album covers, modeling shoots, actor studio sessions, and photographing concert tours. His use of light, color, posing, and digital effects is creative and innovative, capturing moments in time that feel like a story in a single still image. I had wondered a few times, where would I need to be in life in order to have Jeremy Cowart take my portrait?

Well, turns out, that answer was home. I needed to be home. During a period of quarantine, Jeremy designed a way to connect with his subjects virtually, projecting their image onto a canvas set up in his Nashville studio. He would then backlight the canvas, project various images onto the wall behind it, and use his camera to capture an image of the whole scene. He opened up online sessions to the public, and immediately after I booked a time, I began to practice lighting, background, poses, and outfits with a few friends in order to be ready for my Jeremy Cowart portrait. Steve was among this crew, sharing his opinion about hair, tops, and wearing my favorite hat or not. He was sold on the hat for sure; although I was feeling insecure about it. He has a much bolder sense of style, especially about me, constantly encouraging things that will make both me and my features stand out more boldly than I am often comfortable with. Again, it's the cheerleader thing. He loves and believes in me and wants the whole world to see what he sees. I sometimes want to hide. Steve empowers me to fight that back-seat mindset.

The day of my photo session arrived, and to add more texture to his experience as an artist and to the experience of his social media followers, Jeremy was broadcasting the live virtual photo sessions on his Instastories so people could follow along. When my session time came up, guess which fashion-forward friend of mine was right there following along on Instagram and adding his own flavor in the comments?

While other people asked questions about doing their own session, or praised Jeremy for how cool his work was, my personal hype man had this sequence:

Before it was my turn:
We want KINDLE YES WE DO! (heart emoji)

Once I was on screen:
#teamkindle (fire emoji)
YESSS KINDLE
Put on the hat!!! (three fire emojis)

I couldn't see any of this live at that moment, but when I saw it in the replay later, I laughed with a giddy and full heart. Steve didn't have to think about doing any of that; it just is who he is. But it's also born from the depth of our care and the height of our fun. When I invite Steve to be part of a celebration, I know it will be bigger and more fun because he is there. He makes the journey better.

To thrive on the path of following your fernweh, you need Caelies and Steves. You need people to know the song in your heart. People who have your back, help you celebrate, and cheer you on when you're down. Who this is and how they show up will look different for each of us, so here are some things to think about:

- How do I need to be encouraged on the tough days?
- Who does that well for me?
- When I'm ready to celebrate, who sees me and helps me to honor my growth and accomplishments?
- Who makes it more fun?

The author Jack Canfield says that we "are an average of the five people we spend the most time with." If you put that just in the context of your fernweh community, who are the five people who are the closest to you on this journey? Are they building you up, challenging your beliefs, or teaching you new concepts and skills? If not, make some adjustments to who and where you are investing your time. It's okay to give yourself permission to grow and change. Some folks in your life will struggle with the recalibrating of your relationship. That is also okay. Don't let it slow you down. You've got big dreams and a path of adventure laid out before you.

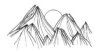

Summary: Guard Steps

- Mind your stuff before someone tries to take off with it or take advantage of you.
- Know your worth and act like it.
- Not everyone needs to be invited in, especially at the beginning.
- Find people who celebrate you and your journey.

PART 5

Expand Your Fernweh

CHAPTER TWENTY-ONE

Sometimes the End is Just the Beginning

We lost my friend Liz to cancer in the early summer, which was also about the time I was entering the last stretch of my travel year. While there were still adventures yet to be had, losing Liz was one of the early trail markers that signaled the big adventure coming to an end. I spent the first part of the summer in the Pacific Northwest, looking at both Portland and Seattle as possible future homes. That part of the United States is glorious in the summer: green, warm, breezy, and light until almost ten o'clock on the longest days. People walk and bike to meet friends for coffee and drinks, lounge in parks in the cities, and find water to play in. There are festivals and food trucks abounding as people emerge from spending a winter inside and revel in every drop of sun and warmth they can before the rain returns. I absolutely adore those two cities, have friends in both, and yet neither was the puzzle piece that fit the next stage of life.

In the spring, I'd started to have a sense in what felt like my gut but what I now have come to understand is my spirit. It was a pull, a sense of clarity, about the East Coast that I mentioned earlier. Which made absolutely no sense, being so far from my West Coast home, family, and friends, and even farther away from my brother and family in Japan. So, I'd set it to the side and continued to look at West Coast options. The more I narrowed them down to a few finalists, the less things fit together.

Around this time, my family had made plans to be together in Hawaii at the end of October, which felt like it would be the perfect finale to this season of adventure, just about fourteen months after it began. As I continued to talk with God in the spring about what was coming after this fernweh year, he gave me a picture in my head of a moment in Hawaii that hadn't yet happened. In this image, we were all by the ocean at sunset on a grassy area leading down toward the beach, enjoying a champagne toast as the sun went down. I loved it, it was beautiful and calming, but it came and went quickly, not something I held on to for long.

The travel had begun to wear on me. It was becoming routine and monotonous to pack every few weeks, visit a new city, and explore by myself. I was lonely for a community and jealous for a place that was my own. I missed my dog and my friends more and more each trip. The time was quickly approaching to come off the road and to decide which city I would call home. I had mostly settled on San Diego since I had always wanted to live there. At the same time I was mulling over where to land, my manager gave me a bit longer to decide on a location, and a friend offered me her San Diego house to stay in while she and her family were traveling. I could take the pup along for this trip and be there for almost a month, giving me the chance to see what real life might be like in that city.

I celebrated my next birthday there with friends, feeling a sort of unofficial close to the year of travel that had begun with a birthday the year before. I also felt something heavy in the air; change was coming. I'd been in the same industry and with the same company for almost twenty years. I had also begun to realize I was halfway through my career and that there was a lot of professional life still unexplored and unexamined. Especially on the heels of the world exploration and personal growth I'd just spent a year of my life experiencing. Also, in light of so much personal loss and the life reflection and evaluation that comes with the grief.

There was not really a path to stay with the same company, in the same place. I was so grateful for the opportunities that had been afforded to me, but it was time to make a move. I'd had a plan to make a long transition out, and then there were some abrupt changes at work that made it untenable to stay any longer. Shortly after returning home from San Diego, in one of the most terrifying and certain decisions I'd made on the entire journey, I left my job with no plan. God had proven to me again and again that when I trusted the sound of his voice, he always had something better. I couldn't yet see the something better that was coming, but I knew his voice was saying it was time, so I followed.

I said goodbye to a world I'd known for almost two decades, and less than a week later, I boarded my flight to the Hawaiian island of Kauai. What I previously thought would be a vacation to punctuate an adventure became a journey to demarcate an era. Uncertainty, grief, terror, freedom, potential, and glee swirled around in every moment during those days. It was a fight to stay fully present as I did my very best to focus on time with my family. My niece was in that super sweet place of being four and wanting to do everything I did. We had dance parties, swam, colored, and played games. She wanted to sit next to me at meals, hold my hand when we walked places, and hang with me on the pool loungers. It was the actual best.

I took some time to decompress and process the last year or so on my own, too, giving myself permission to move slowly in the world, take walks on my own, get a massage, and read. We went to a luau, cooked meals together, and stopped at a fruit stand for local mangos. It was a very low-key and slow-moving vacation, exactly as needed. We decided to have one night out at a nice place at the end of the trip, my dad leaving it up to me to find something, knowing his daughter by far had the best eye for this type of thing. I'd seen a friend mention a place they'd been for a special dinner on Kauai with their family recently, so I grabbed a reservation there, working with the hostess to get a table by the windows.

We all dressed up a bit. I wore a new bright pink dress that felt celebratory and fabulous, demonstrating both how I felt and how I was trying to convince myself to feel. We walked in the restaurant's front door, through the foyer, and were taken to our table on the far side of the dining room, past floor-to-ceiling windows and open sliding doors, which looked out over a vast lawn sprawling down a slope to the sand and the beach. The sun was just about to hit the beginning of golden hour, warm and streaming in through the windows to our table.

Instantly, I almost froze in my steps as I realized this was the place that God had shown me, the image I'd seen in my mind almost half a year before. He knew this is where I would be, both geographically and on my fernweh journey. All those months ago, he was telling me that he had me. He'd given me a preview of this place so that when I got here, it wouldn't be scary but familiar and comforting. On one of the last nights of the year of adventure, reveling in the finale trip and uncertain of what was to come, he was showing me that this was actually just the beginning.

So I ordered a glass of champagne and toasted to a great trip, to an incredible year of opportunity, and to the hope of what was to come. And then I dragged my family out onto that lawn for an overabundance of pictures in the golden-hour light. The French call it *l'heure magique*, the magic hour. That moment was pure magic. God was doing something in my heart and soul, something that could never be unraveled or undone.

Sometimes what feels like the end is really just the start of something new. If it is hard for you to imagine anything beyond your present circumstances, hang in there. There is always hope, always a chance to begin again. There is poetry in the Bible that talks about how everything in life has a season. Whether you realize it or not, your new beginning is coming. That's how fernweh works, after all. Right when you think you've reached the end, the drumbeat starts beating once again.

CHAPTER TWENTY-TWO

Everything Can Change

Turns out the year that I thought would change things up a bit changed everything. When I left the old life completely behind at the end of the fernweh year, I asked God, *In my next job, can you have the whole world be open to me?* Audacious, perhaps even a bit too bold. But, in fact, God wasn't done with the adventure. As I researched and considered my next opportunity and next city, there was so much to be deeply grateful for. I had family and friends who supported me and helped me find my way, find myself again after so much change. My travels continued and even included a vacation to Mexico. I was able to grow a personal consulting business and support myself despite being off work for almost nine months. I wrote my prayers in my journal:

I want this next phase of my life to be full of a hope and a future. You have given me the dream of following my fernweh, of being an international citizen, and it seems the best way to do that is to go after it with all I have. You have provided so, so much for me during this time! I am so grateful!

I'd been thinking most seriously about San Diego as my next home, and I had some great leads on roles there. But it felt like I was forcing something into that timeline, like I wasn't listening to what God was really saying to me about what was next. I had lunch with a friend in the Bay Area one day, and she suggested a company where her daughter worked. She thought I'd really enjoy the mission and culture. *The one in Boston?* I thought. *I'm not moving to Boston. I've never even been to Boston.* Yet, I remembered that sense from the previous spring, a sense I'd had about my next city being on the East Coast.

So I wrote the name of the company on a piece of paper and shoved it in my purse while we had lunch, only to pull it out and look at it a few weeks later. I set it on a side table, where it stayed for a few more weeks, and then I finally peeked at it and googled the company. She was right. It absolutely fit what I was looking for next. I found their careers site—couldn't hurt to just look, after all. Within minutes, I found a role that perfectly described my strengths and experience. So I wrote a cover letter and applied without overthinking it, a worrisome habit now broken by almost two years of making imperfect decisions toward unknown destinations. Something about this place drew me to take the next step. Within a few weeks, we were scheduling an initial phone call, that led to a video call, that led to an interview trip to Boston.

I loved the people immediately; they felt like "my people." But I couldn't get past the idea of relocating to a city I'd only just visited for the first time, past the idea of starting over, or even how I would care for my dog while I was at work. So I paused the conversations with Boston and continued with my California options, which were delightful and amazing options. They just still didn't feel right for the time. You may also know that feeling of when something is good on paper, but it's just not quite right. I would wake up each day thinking about the place I'd interviewed with in Boston and the people I'd met along the way. I finally came to a place where I told God I needed a definitive answer so I could let it go.

May 11th

I'm still fussing about Boston. I would see it as an adventure. A chance for life to get bigger and bolder at each turn. Boston would be amazing for the work and for the opportunity. I am trying to talk myself into getting brave.

May 27th

I am scared. But I'm more scared of trying something too small and being bored than having a 'too big' feeling.

I wrote this journal entry on the Saturday of Memorial Day weekend, where I also wrote that I needed to make a final decision by Monday, just two days away. I went to church the next day, and after church, a few of us went into the cute downtown of the city for the annual strawberry festival. The streets were blocked off to allow for artisan and food vendor stalls. People milled about in the sun, bumping into friends, neighbors, and familiar faces. Little did I know more fruit would come of that day than just strawberries.

I was talking with some friends when another group of ladies walked up to join us, one of them wearing the brightly colored T-shirt of the company I had interviewed with in Boston. Literally the exact same company I asked for a sign about by the next day and there it was. I emailed them the following morning.

This time, I went wholeheartedly into the conversation with Boston, and within three months, was driving the pup and our belongings across the country to our new home. Remember the ask I had of God, that my next opportunity would open up the whole world? The place he led me to in Boston literally touches all seven continents with its products and services. He multiplied my dream of experiencing far-off places by taking me to yet another far-off place. I arrived for my first day of work with a packed suitcase and my passport in hand. After meeting all my coworkers and getting the first-day administrative things handled, I left the office to catch an overnight flight to Paris for my first work trip. That day was just the beginning of new and bigger adventures than even the year of fernweh travel provided.

I've walked the halls of palaces in Spain and France, visited castles in Bavaria and Portugal, ridden on a gondola under the Bridge of Sighs and a water taxi in the snow on the Grand Canal in Venice. I've sampled Christmas market glühwein to my heart's delight, floated on the river under the evening lights of the Eiffel Tower, walked high above the Thames River inside the Tower Bridge, and strolled and tasted my way through dozens of new cities in Europe.

The opportunity to see the world is just the normal culture in my professional experience now. I've often wondered how silly the passing conversations in the halls and elevators would sound to someone from the outside. Seeing a colleague after a few weeks of absence or trying to schedule a catch-up lunch involves a running list of the travel we've all been doing and where we are headed next. It's an embarrassment of riches, to be sure, except that I'm not at all embarrassed. I am blessed and grateful.

Hand in hand with the incredible places and experiences are the people who have come into my life along the path in my new home city: open minded, adventurous, authentic, curious, and passionate about culture and personal growth. People who share my faith and those who are happy that I'm happy about my faith. These fellow wayfinders have helped me grow, break old patterns and mindsets, and create a life full of more potential than I'd seen before. Some I've shared space with for a few hours, some a few days, and some are in my life now for the duration.

Each one of these people and experiences is a gift, and not lost on me is the simple truth that had I pushed to the side the crazy dream that popped up in my journal one random January day over two years earlier, none of them would have been mine. In the Old Testament, there is a verse that feeds my soul. I shared it earlier in this book. God says:

Look at the nations and watch—and be utterly amazed. For I am going to do something in your days that you would not believe, even if you were told.

Habakkuk 1:5

I have been utterly amazed on this fernweh journey. With each new experience and incredible person added to my life, my heart gets a bit fuller, not just from what I've lived, but with the reminder of how good God is and how much he loves our dreams. He made us, you and me, to dream big dreams. He made us to hear the call of things that are far away, things we can only see with his help to get us there and our own willingness to follow that call. It can be scary, even terrifying, and most definitely uncertain. But the astounding things God shows us and blesses us with, not just at the end of the journey, but also along the way, are worth every trembling step.

CHAPTER TWENTY-THREE

Calling us to Ourselves

Reading back through my journals leading up to the year of travel, I see that girl; I understand her feelings, her fears, and her thought processes. I know why she thought what she thought and felt what she did. I see the dreams far away, and also the doubt and reasoning for why they wouldn't be possible. All of the, *But how could I? But what if it . . . ? What if it doesn't? What if it does?* The lies, the hesitation, the lack of confidence, and the lack of boundaries. I see that girl, but I don't know her anymore. I'm not her anymore.

In contrast, when I read the words of the woman who experienced a year of travel, growth, love, and heartbreak, the woman who left her job, the woman who no longer tolerated the oppression of dreams, emotion, and potential, I know that woman. She is the same person who speaks today. That is the start of who I am now and yet absolutely not the end of who I am becoming.

What I thought would be a fun year, a year of adventure, a self-contained experience, was in fact a rudder that changed the course of my life. It meant I was no longer willing to be the best gal pal, the supporting actress in my own life. It meant I reprioritized how I spent my time, what I invested in emotionally, and who and what I let into my life and my heart.

Giving myself permission to say yes to that one crazy thought about a year of travel was the start of it all. Did I go directly from idea to jetway? No way.

You see it all now that we've talked about it. It was:

The idea.

Asking what questions would need to be answered:

- What would I really want out of it?
- Who needs to get on board?
- Who needs to be left out for a while?
- What pieces need to be in place?
- In what order?
- What is the timeline?
- Where is God in all of this?

I had to be okay with:

- Being misunderstood.
- Being alone.
- Being envied.

- Being judged.
- Being uncertain.
- Embracing the uncertainty.
- Self-starting.
- Getting lost.

I had to let go of:

- Expectations.
- Timelines.
- Comfort.
- Codependency.
- Approval.
- Control.

Doing something like this, you develop a confidence in yourself that cannot be undone. You develop a quest for authenticity that cannot be undone. An aspect of life I find heartbreaking, especially for women, is this idea of "should." We have so many expectations around gender, age, faith, vocation, family, just to scratch the surface. The cultural expectation for each of these sets out a framework, but how often do we move down the track in that framework without allowing ourselves to ask if this is even what we want to be doing?

We might ask ourselves, "Am I happy?" And then affirm for ourselves, "Yes, with the life I have, I am happy. I am content."

But what if your life could get so much bigger and louder? What if you allow yourself to look inside first and really be authentic with yourself about that dream that you've shoved down into the back of your heart? For me, that dream was the world. For you, it might be art, a business, a relationship, a path of service, a new career course, a family, a home, or a new rhythm of life.

What would happen if you gave yourself permission to explore that crazy idea you've had? Did you ever see that movie *Julie and Julia*? It's the story of a gal who enjoyed cooking and needed a big, audacious goal to chase after. So she decided to cook every recipe from Julia Child's *Mastering the Art of French Cooking* over the course of one year. As an aspiring writer, part of her yearlong journey would include blogging about the recipes.

Did she bite off more than she could chew? (Pun, of course, intended.) Absolutely. Were there days she was overwhelmed, obsessed, stressed, disappointed, and confused? Yes. But look at what came from it. Every day she recommitted to herself, put herself first, held on to a tiny hope that she could complete something hard and audacious. She had some key people around her who supported her, and while they may not have understood her need to do what she did, they believed in her and encouraged her to complete the challenge. They celebrated her when it worked and backed her up when it didn't.

The relationship with herself and her core people grew stronger. She ended the year a person of accomplishment, who does the hard work every day to commit to achieving a goal. She inspired and entertained others. Oh, and she ended up with a book and a movie deal. But would it all have been worth it if the only impact was on herself as a human? It sure would have. That is enough. She was enough of a reason, all on her own.

CHAPTER TWENTY-THREE

You, also, are reason enough. Just you.

Now, you might be having some feelings about this right now. You might be silently telling me that I'm crazy. You're thinking about the impact following your fernweh might have on your family, your work, your free time, and your commitments. You've already thought about the naysayers' voices and your own self-doubt. Yes, okay, I hear that. And I say, just for this moment, tell those worries, doubts, and potential opinions from other people to *shhh*. Literally put your finger to your lips and symbolically shush them if you need to.

Set aside the reasons why your fernweh could not possibly be what you think it is, why it won't work, why it's not possible, and why you can't even allow yourself to dream. Turn your heart, your mind, and your spirit to what's possible. Open yourself up to the idea that you were designed with a passion, ability, or dream that's unique to you. Just for this next little bit together, tune your heart to hear the drumbeat of a dream that you haven't explored in a while, and be open to where that sound might take you.

This might be a good time to have a journal handy, perhaps even your Bible if that's a helpful guide for you. I am praying for this next part of the fernweh conversation that you will find fresh ideas about old dreams and new ideas you've never seen before. My hope is that you see your life as it was intended: full of prom-ise, hope, and joy. And that your fernweh drumbeat begins to get louder.

You've heard my personal fernweh experience, culminating in a year of travel around the world, and then a move across the coun-try. I've asked you some reflection questions along the way. Now, will you allow me to walk you through a few directed steps that may help you find and follow your own fernweh? If you already know what your fernweh is, perhaps these steps will aid you in conversations with the people in your own life who are trying to uncover theirs.

Let's do this one step at a time. Close your eyes, and while they are closed, tell any thoughts of self-doubt to shush. Focus on when you have been capable, when the possibilities actually started to happen, when things worked out and fell into place. If you're struggling, take some long, deep breaths. Breathe all the way into your diaphragm and abdomen. Take a few long breaths like that. If you pray, pray. Ask for help to clear your mind. When the doubt and nerves have quieted down or even left you for a bit, open your eyes again and we'll do the next thing.

Now, with a clear heart and mind, ask yourself—and ask God, if that applies—some of these questions:

- What is an idea that, when I think about it, my heart beats a little faster?
- What is the desire in my heart that lingers there that I push to the side?
- What is the drumbeat of my soul that has been steady in the background, or continues to get louder each day, each week, each year that goes by?
- What is the thing that I have pushed into the back of my heart and mind but just can't bring myself to let go of altogether?

Close your eyes and just ask. A clear picture may come into focus, or just a blurry sense of something. Either is okay. Whatever you get, let it linger there for a bit. Let the idea expand into some *what ifs*.

That. That idea or topic right there. That just might be your fernweh.

Before it slips away again, retreating behind all the reasons why not, write it down. Put it right here in this book, in a note on your phone, a sticky on your mirror, or in your journal. Right now, capture it. We aren't doing anything else with it today. We are just letting it be itself. Let it have a little light, air, and space to play. Your job is to protect it—from doubt, from critique, from you, and from others. We are in the discovery space. Let it be a wonder to you for now.

My personal process is that, in this stage, what I'm discovering is only for me and God. I don't share this space with any other human, for the reasons we spoke about earlier. You may be different in that you have one person, a spouse or a best friend, that you let into spaces like this. You do what works for you. Just make sure that it actually is working for you.

You may be reading this knowing you have found the general thing you are passionate about but haven't found a way to channel it yet. That is perfectly fine; it's a journey. What a perfectly delightful place to be, still growing and discovering. You can know your fernweh and not know all the places it will possibly take you. The element of surprise along the journey will be a big part of the fun.

CHAPTER TWENTY-FOUR

The Why

We hear a lot of talk about understanding your "why." As someone who has spent a portion of my career in sales, this is a powerful tool to not only explain your product or service, but to understand the customer's motivation and tap into that to get them to engage with you. This, however, is not that. You are not selling anyone on your fernweh, including yourself, because you have already bought in.

Identifying the *why* of your fernweh does two key things for you:

1. Gives you a north star to come back to.
2. Helps you prioritize.

Your reason for your fernweh can be anything. It can be as big and bold as "because it will change the country I grew up in for generations to come," or as lighthearted as "because it will make me and other people laugh." We need both. God created diplomats and comedians, engineers, and entertainers. We need it all.

If you can get past the need to judge your own motivation, then you will absolutely start to not care when others judge it also. And, oh, they will. For sure, you will be judged. If you are someone who struggles with navigating the judgment of others, working through that is going to be part of your fernweh journey. You will be blessed to come to a place of realizing that when people judge, it's really themselves who need some care. Share this book with them when you're done. Perhaps it will help them, too. Because you know what Brené Brown says, right?

If you're not in the arena also getting your ass kicked, I'm not interested in your feedback.

You will need a *why* during many days and moments along your fernweh journey. You will have glorious, exciting days when everything is falling into place, affirming your reason for following your fernweh. You will have days when this feels like the worst thing you have ever done and you want to give up and walk away. Both of these, and everything in between, are why you need your *why* to come back to for both celebration and for motivation.

You also need to understand your *why* so you can prioritize what comes your way in this process. For me, there were many opinions about which cities to visit and where to go. When I came back to my why—I wanted to experience as many new places and people as possible in my year, as well as explore potential new home cities—it helped me make decisions about where to go next. It allowed me to look at places I might not have considered and to take opportunities off the list that didn't align.

So now, the practical.

Go back to where you wrote your fernweh down. Pick it back up and enjoy it for a minute. Remember that feeling in your heart, mind, and soul you had when you let it loose. Get back to that.

Now, ask yourself, *Why?*

- Why do you want to follow this thing?
- What will be the value added for you?
- What will be the value added for others?

Write that *why* down. Don't edit it, judge it, or truncate it. Just let it be. If there is more than one reason, totally fine. Get all the *whys* down.

Now take a break. Take a deep breath, and step away. Walk through the world for the rest of today as if you are doing this thing. Try it on for size and see how it feels. Notice if you feel lighter, more hopeful, and more empowered. If you do, then it's still your fernweh. Does it scare you a bit? It could still be your fernweh.

If it feels like a burden or dreadful, it's not your fernweh. Go back and try again. Fernweh can feel big, even scary, but not burdensome. That's where the "should" lives, not the "what if."

Now it's time to get practical again. You've let yourself try this idea on for a few conversations. You've let it out in the open, had a dance with it, seen that it's actually more fun than you thought it was, right? You have a clearer understanding of why you want to pursue your fernweh.

Yet, there are still challenges or obstacles that get in the way. Questions that are left unanswered. It's time to face those. What questions or obstacles get in the way of why you want to follow your fernweh? How can you answer these questions and get past the obstacles?

It's okay to let some of those challenges come back so you can face them. However, they are not allowed to create doubt. These are the questions of practicality, and they are permitted to come back so you can look them in the face and find a solution. Let me share with you some of the questions I had to answer for my fernweh year:

- Where do I want to go?
- Where will I stay when I'm not traveling?
- How will I stay connected to my friends?
- What will happen with my dog while I travel?
- Where will I put my belongings, my house stuff, and my furniture?

Write down your own logistical questions. If you capture them on paper, they aren't as scary. Ready, set, make your list.

Okay, are you back? Did you have the same thought I did when I tried this exercise? *Oh, that's it? Okay, these all have solutions. Let's do this.* If the answer is not that easy, then start with one challenge that needs a solution and investigate what's possible. You won't solve every question you have in one sitting. Some may take research, and some may take conversations. To that end, the next bit of practicality is: Who needs to buy into this?

You may need other people to buy into your fernweh because you need an inner circle of support, you need approval for a certain piece to fall into place, or you're about to change the way of life for the people you live with and care about.

For me, I needed some logistical yeses. Part of my plan was to keep working while I traveled. I mean, somebody was going to need to pay for all that cheese and wine in Europe and ya girl had just four weeks of vacation in a year. I needed my manager to be on board. My job was overseeing offices in the western U.S., so as long as I had my computer and a phone, I could work from anywhere. The culture was very focused on being in the office, so I asked to be able to work from a space in offices around the country while I explored new cities with the intent to find a place to eventually settle in.

It was nerve-wracking to ask for this. If this piece was a no, it was probably a non-starter. So I laid out my reasoning, including how it would benefit the organization as a whole, and then asked, "So, what do you think?" As you already know, the response was even better than expected. Not only was my manager supportive, but by the time the year of travel started, the regions had been moved around so I would oversee offices on both coasts, and eventually London. An even greater outcome than I could have imagined.

The other person I needed buy-in from was my mom. She'd been renting my room out to grad students for years, so taking in a boarder wasn't new for her. I would be in and out all the time, coming and going. Mostly needing a place to sleep, do laundry, and get my mail. For that whole year, I was never home more than three weeks in a row, and that was around Christmastime. Now, as many moms do, she wanted the best for me and she worried. So I was expecting to have to answer a lot of practical questions, then she'd think about it, then she'd have some terms and conditions, and then we'd agree on it. But she was all in, feet first from the start. I can still remember the smile she had when I asked her to be part of this adventure in this way. Did we still need to talk about the logistics? Of course. She had expectations of me just like any of her housemates, and we worked out a weekly rental rate for when I was home. But she was in.

Those two ladies catching the vision were the on-ramps for so much of this adventure. And I was able to approach them more confidently because I knew my *why*. I knew the purpose behind following my fernweh. I am forever grateful that God allowed them to see the potential in it with me, to understand my *why*. And he did; he made a way. Was it scary to even ask? Terrifying. But you know what, the answer is always a no unless we ask. I'm a firm believer that it's good to get comfortable with hearing "no," as that helps us get over our fear of asking in the first place.

CHAPTER TWENTY-FIVE

Celebrate Others

At the start of the 2020s, the world began talking a lot about empathy. Not sure what took us so long to get there, but we finally did. Google defines empathy as "the ability to understand and share the feelings of another." This becomes especially important when we look at issues of social justice, poverty, abuse, discrimination, sexism, gender bias, gender identity, and power dynamics. Often the feelings that need to be empathized with are negative feelings someone or a group has experienced under negative circumstances. We have to both see them through our eyes and turn the prism and see their lived experience through their eyes.

One day, while thinking about empathy, it struck me that much of what we hear are reminders to approach folks empathetically when it comes to the challenging situations and the negative experiences they've had in their lives: the hardship, heartache, negativity, or injustice. It struck me that I couldn't remember hearing about having empathy toward the positive experiences in someone's life. Empathy toward their joys, their successes, their blessings, and their delights.

This feels like a good place to get real for a second. Among women, when another woman has a life situation to be celebrated, sometimes that joy is met with jealousy, envy, gossip, friction, control, or judgment. For some reason, women can immediately see another woman's wins as commentary on what they don't have. We envy it, feel threatened by it, and then try to put it in its place. Does every woman do this? Absolutely not, thank God. But there is an undercurrent of this; it does exist.

How many of us have even once been part of conversations gossiping about someone's wedding, home decor, career, appearance, spouse, children, or life choices? Whether we have been the ringleader of the discussion or a passive observer, we are complicit in tearing the subject down rather than celebrating them.

What would help us turn this tension around and instead celebrate women in all our amazingness? I submit to you, it's empathy. Specifically, empathy about the positive in someone's life. What if instead of meeting someone's success or excitement with our own doubt, fears, judgement, and general naysaying, we turned the prism and looked at their wins from their perspective? What if we imagined the feelings of excitement they are having, and maybe even had empathy enough to acknowledge they could still be battling a thin layer of self-doubt? What if we celebrated each other? Like, literally throw a party and pop champagne for big life things: when a woman we know gets a promotion, finishes teaching school for the year, hits a personal record in their fitness goals, publishes their first blog post, finishes their back deck project, or hits a milestone number of followers on their business accounts.

The cool thing about empathy is it sets aside the value *we* put on someone's wins and helps us to see why *they* value it. When we can do that, then we can truly value them and celebrate them. Let me share a simple example. A few years back, my friend Anna got into running as a way to focus her health and fitness goals. She started running 5Ks, then 10Ks, then half marathons, and eventually a marathon. She said she was never the fastest on the course, but she always pushed herself and she always finished.

Then one year, she decided her goal for that year was to run one thousand miles in the year. One thousand miles. That may not seem like a big deal for that span of time, but to hit that goal, she'd need to run just under three miles per day, every day of the year, no days off. The no-days-off thing wasn't realistic, so she'd need to have days that were longer, leaving room for injury and recovery days, too.

To have some big running days, she chose a few long running events throughout the year, and then built her run calendar around that, filling in the weeks and months around the longer distance events. (Is this calendar planning thing sounding familiar?) She was on track to finish by mid-December but hit a mental wall a month or so out. We were talking about it one day, and I asked, "What if we make the last mile a party night? Then you have a target to keep chasing and a due date to hit. Would you be into that?"

Anna loved this and seemed to leave our call with a little more excitement to finish the thousand miles. Sure enough, one weeknight in December, a bunch of us met up at the local track to cheer her on for her last mile. She saved one mile, four laps around the track, for this moment with friends. We cheered her as she started to run the first few steps, and we cheered her each time she finished a lap and passed by us.

Who knew what people thought of us that night? As Anna rounded the corner on her fourth lap, we got *loud* on the edge of that track. We had a sign that read, "You did it! 1,000 miles!" and we held a streamer across the track that she broke through like a finish line. We crowned her head with a plastic party store crown, and then we took her for Mexican food and margaritas.

It was completely frivolous and completely full of value. By celebrating our friend, we showed her that what was important in her life was important in ours, too. We showed empathy.

Honoring someone's fernweh takes a ton of empathy, especially when it's just at the beginning. It's easier to celebrate someone when the big goal is done. True empathizers can also celebrate the dream, the start, the process, and the learning.

I shared earlier about how my brother came home from two years in Japan to promptly turn around and join the Peace Corps in Zambia. What I didn't know at the time was that he was following his fernweh.

Only a few months after returning from Japan, he was itching to get back out in the world. For a long time, he'd had his own drumbeat to join the Peace Corps, and he started talking about it more and more after returning home.

He called one day to get my advice. On a break from a conference I was attending, I stepped outside the front entrance to return his call. The wind was blowing hard across an open field to where I was, and I had to tuck into a little corner outside the building to have what continues to be, for me, one of the most sacred conversations in our relationship. He'd been accepted into the Peace Corps, and he told me about agonizing over whether to go or not. Two years. Africa. Community fish farming.

As his sister, I was terrified and feeling selfish. Nothing in me wanted him to be away from us, to be in a challenging and far-away part of the world. He had just barely gotten back from Japan. Hadn't he gotten living across an ocean out of his system? Why did he need to go away again, to leave again? I wanted him nearby so we could be adults together, do life together as siblings.

All these feelings swirled around in my heart and mind, when I started to actually listen and to hear him. To hear *his* heart, and his fernweh, although I would not have called it that at the time. As we talked through it, all the reasons he gave for wanting to stay close to home were about outside pressures.

He talked about how, if he left for two years and came home, all his friends would be years ahead in their personal lives and their careers. Then he talked about all the reasons he wanted to go, and his countenance changed palpably, even over the phone. You could hear it; the energy lifted, there was hope and potential in how he spoke, and as I heard his excitement, what rang in my mind was a quote a friend once shared: "To love someone is to learn the song in their heart and to sing it to them when they have forgotten."

With all the outside noise, my brother called because he couldn't hear his song anymore. The drumbeat of his fernweh had become too faint for him to hear it clearly and match its rhythm. In that moment, I realized there was a choice to make. I could have silenced his drumbeat for this adventure, potentially forever, feeding into the fear, doubt, the safe option, and well-worn path. I was afraid for his safety and afraid of losing him. Which could happen; there was no guarantee of a positive outcome. Or he could stay here, and I would lose him anyway. We would all lose him to the land of mediocrity and dreams cast aside for practicality's sake. A part of him would be lost if he stayed here where it was familiar.

"You should go," I said.

And he did. And I was anxious for two and a half years until he came home.

This is where I tell you that he got the international thing out of his system, he's home in the States these days, and we live down the street from each other, right? You already know that it isn't. He was home for less than a year and went back to Japan, where he married a gal he couldn't stop thinking about since living there, and built a life and a business, and I have a gorgeous niece and nephew who are half American by heritage and fully Japanese by culture. That's the thing with fernweh. Once someone finds their path, they usually continue to see where it goes. As they should, and we can help to fuel that fire for them.

When you see someone else struggling to hold on to their dream, to hear the drumbeat deep in their heart, do you sing them their song, or do you hit pause until they can't hear it anymore?

Let's chat for a second.

CHAPTER TWENTY-FIVE

- Who needs your empathy and your celebration when it comes to their dream?
- Who is just getting started and needs a milestone celebrated?
- Who learned a big lesson or leveled up in some way and would have the encouragement they need to chase the next goal just through a text, call, kind word, card, or flowers dropped on a doorstep?
- Who is about to launch or finish something that has been a longtime dream, and now it's time to *party*?!

How are you going to celebrate these voyagers in your life?

In turn, do you let others into your space to celebrate you? This is the one I struggle with the most. I know how much it means to be able to honor the people we love and their accomplishments, and yet I'm the worst at letting others do this for me. If you're the same, revisit the chapter about getting you a cheering squad.

Part of following your fernweh is not just accepting celebration, but learning to celebrate others around you. We all need the encouragement, especially in our pursuit of dreams. Fernweh will always draw us back to others.

CHAPTER TWENTY-SIX

Expect to Have an Impact

There is a beautiful quote that is often attributed to Nelson Mandela in his inauguration speech, but the source is actually author Marianne Williamson. She says:

Our deepest fear is not that we are inadequate. Our deepest fear is that we are powerful beyond measure. It is our light, not our darkness, that most frightens us. We ask ourselves, "Who am I to be brilliant, gorgeous, talented, fabulous?" Actually, who are you not to be? You are a child of God. Your playing small does not serve the world. There is nothing enlightened about shrinking so that other people won't feel insecure around you. We are all meant to shine, as children do. We were born to make manifest the glory of God that is within us. It's not just in some of us; it's in everyone. And as we let our own light shine, we unconsciously give other people permission to do the same. As we are liberated from our own fear, our presence automatically liberates others.

There are two lines which stand out to me from this quote, and even echo in my mind at times: "Your playing small does not serve the world," and "we unconsciously give other people permission to do the same." Both of these lines have something powerful in common in that they share the message that the purpose of our gifts, talents, and experiences lies in their impact on other people—in service to others, even.

The quote is so good because it starts by addressing our insecurities, then embracing our power, and then ending with the impact on—dare we say liberation of?—others. It echoes much of what Biblical writings teach us, specifically what Paul writes about in some of his letters to the early churches.

In Galatians, Paul writes, "It is for freedom that Christ has set us free" (Galatians 5:1). And in Ephesians, he writes, "Now to him who is able to do immeasurably more than all we ask or imagine, according to his power that is at work within us, to him be glory in the church and in Christ Jesus throughout all generations, for ever and ever! Amen" (Ephesians 3:20–21).

Think for a moment about what the author was saying, that God can do more than we can ever dream of and that him doing these great things is actually for his glory to shine through our lives for all time. Couple that with the idea that each of us is a unique and created being, knit together from before we took our first breath by a creator who loves us, who created us to enjoy both the process and the outcome. I think we have some solid ground to stand on for getting bold and going after our fernweh. It grants permission to change the internal narrative from *I could never do that* to *Why couldn't I do that?* Even beyond the impact on ourselves, changing our own internal narrative, then acting on our new foundation of belief changes the atmosphere for those around us. As we are set free, unloosed to pursue that pounding drumbeat in our spirit, we set others free to do the same.

In the beginning of my fernweh year, the two biggest reactions that came my way about the journey ahead were excitement or skepticism. As I moved through the year, sharing pictures and stories of adventures, sharing the joys and the lessons I was learning, there was a shift to curiosity and even longing on the part of others. By the end, I started to hear and see tangible outcomes in others' lives.

I saw folks in my circle, who had been following along for the journey, leaving soul-sucking jobs, pursuing music, and even moving abroad. One friend said directly to me, "Seeing you travel the world has inspired us to get out there and travel more as a family." These unexpected developments became a highlight of the whole experience. The personal growth was sweet, but just as sweet was witnessing the courage of others who were inspired because I followed my fernweh.

As you read this, you might be wrestling with a monologue of inner doubt. The usual topics for this one include:

- *What could I possibly have to offer others?*
- *Aren't people focused on their own lives and not paying attention to what I am up to?*
- *Can just living my life actually impact how someone else lives theirs?*

One of the best ways to work through these doubts is to create some space for reflection. Look back on conversations you've had with people in your life both personally and professionally. Think about when someone has shared that you have made a difference for them or had an impact on their life. Think about when your strength in an area has been observed or celebrated, perhaps a skill someone else said they wished they possessed or could improve in. The memories you are recalling now could be clues to help you uncover your passion and drumbeat from the build-up of self-doubt.

Give yourself permission to push past all the doubt and hear what is true: you were put on this earth at this exact time in history to make a difference in the lives of others. Admittedly, I've got no empirical evidence to back this up, but in my experience, when someone is following their fernweh, there is a ripple effect of positive impact on those around them.

As I told others about my travels and how the year of fernweh originally came to be, even years after the one big year of travel was over, the reactions have been consistently the same. People smile in joy at the idea of it, they ask questions, they want to know more, and they often tell me they are inspired. When you live your adventure, your passion, your dream, and you try things, make mistakes, and get up and keep going, you encourage others to do the same. It might be one person or thousands, but your life and your journey will impact others.

As I've refined and shared the idea that fernweh is so much more than a physical destination, but that it is also the call of something longed for and not yet discovered, it's become clear how deeply it resonates with so many people. It's also become clear that I want to share it with others. As I reflected on what a fernweh journey looks like from the beginning, I also began to discover that we just might have more than one fernweh rhythm in our lives. Some may have many. I now know that I have at least two.

When the world came to a halt during a global pandemic, I did what most people did. I made sourdough while lounging in my yoga pants. That lasted for a few loaves and then I killed my batch, so that was done. I did many of the distractions that others did, had some heartbreak and some quiet moments with God. I learned to truly enjoy the slower pace, my own company, and being without constant distraction. And when I was finally quiet, and attentive, and looking to God for what he truly had for me in this season, he reminded me of a fernweh drumbeat that had been around since I was a child. It had come up again, during the same period of time that I was beginning to dream about the year of travel. As I imagined being on the road a few years earlier, I wrote about it in my journal. I also wrote another dream for that year:

"Write a book and find a publisher."

I journaled a lot in the time leading up to the year of travel and while I was on the road, processing both experiences and emotions. What I didn't do was write about it like a travel journal. It was too precious of a season to give time away from living it to writing about it, so I stayed completely engaged in each day, embracing the year as loudly as I could. As you already know, the end of the year brought so much change that I set the writing and the dream of a book to the side.

Along with the timing being off, somehow the idea of writing a book was much scarier than traveling solo for a year. There isn't really much to fail at with travel. You make plans, pack a bag, get to your flight on time, see amazing things, eat new delights, encounter engaging people, and you come home. The journey is all mine, to enjoy, to experience, to decide the value of it to me. With a book, it is putting your thoughts, your skill, and a bit of yourself out there for others to experience. For others to review, to decide if it's good or bad.

Like moving to Boston, however, the idea of a book would not leave me alone until it hit me that I would one day carry more regret over never having tried than over someone else's opinion of it. And if you as a reader have made it this far in the book, my hope is that means you found something of value for yourself in these pages. Or you're my mom.

The first fernweh journey is the hardest one, the most awkward, and the most unfamiliar. Taking a leap of faith into something uncertain is one of the most difficult things we can do. Want to know something else? It's also the most exhilarating. After my year of travel and after the move to Boston, another professional opportunity with an unknown outcome presented itself. By now, living my life in the unknown has become a much more familiar and even comfortable space. I remember saying to a friend that while God has nothing to prove to me, he has gone out of his way time and again to prove his goodness and faithfulness. To prove that he will always be there when I need him, whether in a dark alley in an unknown city or in the deep recesses of my own heart and soul.

With this new career opportunity, God gave me a visual image of myself standing on the edge of a cliff. In the distance, the sun was descending behind mountain ranges, and nestled in the valley between the mountains and where I stood was a thick layer of fog sitting just below the edge of the cliff. All I could see was a few feet of cliff below and then miles of grayish white dense fog. In the image, I threw my hands and feet in the air like a child off the edge of a pool and jumped, exclaiming, "Catch me, Daddy." And he always has.

The other thing to understand is that the more we take these trusting leaps, the more we reach for big, audacious dreams, the more familiar it becomes. We actually start to change how we see dreams that we perceive as too big or too hard. I love the Henry David Thoreau quote, "Go confidently in the direction of your dreams; live the life you've imagined." What I didn't realize until recently is the full context of that quote, from Thoreau's *Walden*:

I learned this, at least, by my experiment: that if one advances confidently in the direction of his dreams, and endeavors to live the life which he has imagined, he will meet with a success unexpected in common hours. He will put some things behind, will pass an invisible boundary; new, universal, and more liberal laws will begin to establish themselves around and within him; or the old laws be expanded, and interpreted in his favor in a more liberal sense, and he will live with the license of a higher order of beings. In proportion as he simplifies his life, the laws of the universe will appear less complex, and solitude will not be solitude, nor poverty poverty, nor weakness weakness. If you have built castles in the air, your work need not be lost; that is where they should be. Now put the foundations under them.

He, or she, will put some things behind, and will pass an invisible boundary. He, or she, will live with the license of a higher order of things. I think what our dear friend Hank is saying is that we will level up. The more we pursue our dreams, the more we experience what is truly possible, then the more we will no longer settle for mediocre when we have tasted life in the pocket of our dreams.

Do you see how Thoreau ends this? Castles in the air conjures up the image of magnificence in high places, in the heavens. There is no need to bring our aspirations back down to earth; the appropriate place for them is in the high places. Now it is our job to take the steps to make them come true, to put the foundations and the steps under them to build a ladder up to those castles in the sky.

As a person of faith, I also believe in trusting God to help put the foundations under my dreams, that it is not a solo endeavor left only to me. In scripture, 2 Corinthians 3:18 says, "But we all, with unveiled face, beholding as in a mirror the glory of the Lord, are being transformed into the same image from glory to glory, just as from the Lord, the Spirit."

From glory to glory. We are made in his image, and his home is the heavens, where the castles are. As we pursue fernweh, we are reflecting more of his image, his likeness, and his glory. As we follow one fernweh, which may lead to following another one, and then the next one, we experience his wonders and his glory, and we skip from one glory to another one, to the next one.

In the charismatic church, you may often hear folks say the phrase, "More, Lord," meaning more of his presence and more of his goodness in our lives. I recently heard a friend say she had a period of four months where she woke up every day and asked God to make that day better than the day before. What would happen if you and I approached our fernweh journey that way? What would it look like for us to believe that each dream we have could be sweeter and better than the one before? I mean, have you even read Ephesians 3:20?

Now to him who is able to do far more abundantly than all that we ask or think, according to the power at work within us, to him be glory in the church and in Christ Jesus throughout all generations, forever and ever. Amen.

What would it look like for us to live our lives as though this statement is true? To believe in our minds and know in our spirits that God will do more with our lives than we could ever even imagine because of what he has already given us? And for the purpose of showing how amazing he is, not just to the people around you, but for generations to come.

When we follow our fernweh, it changes the atmosphere for us and for those around us. It loosens the ropes from dock ties and grants permission for fellow dreamers and wayfinders to push off in search of a faint call from across the distance. Following your own fernweh will create change within you and around you, change that is inevitable and impossible to ignore. Your impact may just be on one other, or on thousands. But it is almost certain that someone is witness to your dream, and they will be inspired when you choose to follow it.

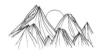

Summary: Expand Steps

- Remember the end is actually the beginning of something more.
- Let everything change.
- Your fernweh will call you closer to yourself than you've ever been.
- Connect to your why and move boldly forward.
- You will empower others.
- Your life will have an impact.

CONCLUSION

This is Not the End

The ironic part about writing a conclusion to a book like this is that this right here is actually just the beginning. For you, that is. My hope and my prayer for you is that something you have found here will ignite a fire in you to get started or get loud with whatever your fernweh is.

Wherever you are in your life, you never have too many years or too little experience to get bold, find courage, and be a little bit foolish in listening to that drumbeat that is deep in your heart. There is never a better time to ask yourself how big and loud can this thing, this life, get? If you silence the doubt and the background noise, your fernweh has probably been calling to you for a while now. If you know it's time, there are a few things I can share.

Things I have found to be true when I followed my fernweh:

- It will be scary.
- There will be people who don't understand it or support it.
- You won't always know what to do.
- You most definitely won't know what's coming next.
- The lingering question, *What if?* will fade into the background.
- The fullness and peace of heart, mind, and soul will begin to silence the other noise.

There is a passage in scripture that comes to mind from Philippians 4:7, "And the peace of God, which surpasses all understanding, will guard your hearts and your minds in Christ Jesus."

As I was nearing the end of the first draft of this book, I told Dr. Taylor, my college roommate, about writing it and about the general concept of following our fernweh. Also a woman of faith, she immediately drew the connection to fernweh and our faith journey. She talked about how, in the end, our one true fernweh, the one that calls to us from deep within our soul over our entire life, is a more meaningful relationship with God. The ultimate calling and longing of our lives is a relationship with him. In the end, that is the most satisfying fernweh journey we can ever take, the only one that will truly satisfy our soul, quiet the noise, and bring us a peace and confidence beyond anything that makes sense through logic or life choices.

Our ultimate fernweh is to follow the sound of the drumbeat of the Creator, who calls to us like the author in the Psalms tells us, "As deep calls to deep." There is nothing more satisfying, profound, or life altering than to follow the sound of his voice. It may sometimes lead us right to the doorstep of our dreams, as you've heard about through my tales and encouragement here in these pages. But it will always lead to ever-ascending heights of peace and joy. And for that reason, the journey will be worth starting and worth staying the course.

So whatever it is, my friend, deep inside you that makes your heart pound heavier at the mere thought of it, I encourage you, today and always, to follow your fernweh.

Acknowledgements

It's a very unique experience, publishing a book at this time in history with the name Kindle. I sometimes have to explain that it is, in fact, my real name. In case you aren't familiar, "kindle" is actually a verb. Per Merriam-Webster online, it means, "to start (a fire) burning; to stir up; to cause to glow." I've come to discover that this word, kindle, is not just my name; it's what I do. I ask hard questions, I help people get started with new ways of thinking and new adventures, I create fun and welcoming spaces and experiences, and I stir things up.

Part of knowing your strengths is also knowing your weaknesses. A friend of mine recently told me that he saw a shirt he plans to buy me that says, "I'm not for everyone." I guess that's what happens when you stir things up. So, I'm especially grateful for the people in my life who are in it together with me and have invested lovingly and honestly along the way.

To my writing people: you inspire, coach, and refine. Thank you for helping a longtime dream come true. Especially to Brett Hilker, who caught this vision from the start and fueled the process with his endless positivity. And to Chelsea Slade, who embraced my voice and pointed to the footholds that would get me to the summit of this climb. (Lady, when are we doing that whiskey?)

To every person who encouraged, cheered from afar, met me in the far-off places on the yearlong travel journey, and who shared how the story of my fernweh inspired and impacted their own fernweh—thank you. Your encouragement helped pave the path that led to these pages.

To the squad of people in my life who know that when you're friends with me, your circle will get bigger and there will probably be wine. And who also know that life with me means we are always in the middle of a conversation—with memes, articles, messages, calls, invites, questions, and ideas from your friend who is always dreaming, planning, and building community. To you, you are the best. You make life sweeter, richer, and more fun. You share your gifts and your inspiration with me, you give me courage, help me laugh at myself, and most importantly, you point me to heaven.

To my mama, who was in this with me from the beginning. Who modeled for me a fierce independence, a willingness to try, and unrivaled planning skills. This would not be in existence without you, Mom.

To my dad and my cousin Lonnie, who picked me up and helped to carry my broken self out of the rubble of a ruined situation so I could start again, thank you. You loaned me your strength and confidence until I found my own again.

To JoJo, my little pup, who was my constant companion through all these adventures, the last being a season of snuggling by his mama's side day after day while she started her dream of writing a book. I miss you, baby boy.

To all the travelers and dreamers who have opened the cover of this book knowing there is something more for you. I count you as fellow wayfinders and am profoundly grateful that you have included me on your journey.

And to those whose lives have inspired me, especially the ones whose stories are found in these pages—you shine like stars. You have illuminated the path ahead so the rest of us can confidently find our footing as we follow our fernweh.

Connect with Kindle

    As you follow your own fernweh, connect with Kindle and share your stories. Let's inspire each other as a community to answer the call from deep within us, and encourage each other when we get stuck along the way. Use #followyourfernweh and #followingmyfernweh when you post on social.

www.followyourfernweh.com
Email: followingmyfernweh@gmail.com
Instagram: @followingmyfernweh
Twitter: @followmyfernweh
Facebook: @KindleSmyth.author

Made in the USA
Las Vegas, NV
09 February 2022